THE MINIATURE PINSCHER

Reigning King of Toys

JACKLYN HUNGERLAND, PH.D.

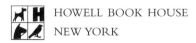

HOWELL BOOK HOUSE

NEW YORK

Howell Book House
IDG Books Worldwide, Inc.
An International Data Group Company
919 E. Hillsdale Boulevard
Suite 400
Foster City, CA 94404

For general information on IDG Books Worldwide's books in the U.S., please call our Consumer Customer Service department at 800-762-2974. For reseller information, including discounts and premium sales, please call our Reseller Customer Service department at 800-434-3422.

Library of Congress Cataloging-in-Publication Data available upon request.

ISBN: 1-58245-141-9

Manufactured in the United States of America
10 9 8 7 6 5 4 3 2 1

Cover and book design by George J. McKeon

Dedication

This book is dedicated to Min Pins everywhere and to the people whom they command.

Acknowledgments

This work could not have been completed without the help and cooperation of the Min Pin breeders and lovers who have shared their personal stories and their treasured archival pictures. Their generosity serves to demonstrate the degree to which they are dedicated to this small, lively and loving breed. My gratitude to them is abundant.

The Miniature Pinscher Club of America has been most generous in sharing data and information, as their goal matches mine—that of bringing the Min Pin to the attention and appreciation of the public.

A special note of appreciation goes to Blake Matheson of Stetson Min Pins, whose support and ability to wring information from a dry well is without equal. Behind Blake lies the support and encouragement of his parents, who have the good sense to realize that this sport—and especially this breed—is Blake's passion. It is within such hands that the future of the Miniature Pinscher will be secure.

Contents

Introduction

I met my first Miniature Pinschers in the early 1950s. Some friends, the Wiltrakises, had outgrown their Boxers and had gotten into this smaller breed that they thought would be less active. Of course they were wrong, and they came to obedience classes where I met them. I watched in admiration as Henrietta Wiltrakis and then Sue Harvey worked with their Min Pins through obedience titles that were hard fought and won! Above all else, I was introduced to the charm and amusement of the breed.

I imagine I first came to the attention of Min Pin breeders when I placed a Min Pin, Ch. Sunbrook Buckskin Gal, second in the Toy Group at the Westminster show in New York. That was in 1990, and the breed and I have been buddies ever since. That same year Buckskin Gal was Best of Breed at the National Specialty.

As a judge I have always been very particular about the kind of Min Pin I prefer. It is generally known that I like the classic, old-style head and that I am a stickler for as good a hackney-like action as I can find among the entries. I have put puppies up to Group wins, and I have passed over some big winners based on whether or not they met my criteria as defined by the breed standard. I have not been a breeder of Min Pins, but I judge every breed as if I am or intend to be a breeder. In other words, I keep the betterment of the breed in the forefront of my thinking when I am judging.

When I was asked to do this book I had a few questions. As I looked at the literature I saw that there are several books about the breed. What, then, was to be special about this book? I was told that this book was to be part of a new series that is intended for the general public as well as the dedicated fancier of a given breed. That is a broad spectrum. It's much easier to focus a publication on a specific segment of readership rather than trying to cover all tastes and interests. However, that was not to be.

When I put out the call for information and pictures and started to research the history and development of the breed, I was met with more than even I thought existed. Fanciers and the Miniature Pinscher Club of America have been extremely generous in sharing their pictures, which present a photographic history of the development of the breed. This enthusiasm stems from the fact that Min Pin fanciers are not fanciers—they are fanatics. They adore their breed and want only the best for their dogs. Because of their attitude, people have been very forthcoming with support for this project.

One thing of particular interest to me as I put the material into manuscript form has been the consistency of this breed. There has been almost a total lack of temporary fads to undermine the breed's basics. The standard has been set since 1980 and for 20 years breeders have protected the essence of breed character for the Min Pin. Yes, two different types have developed, but they are both recognizable as definitively Min Pin. If you were to see only the silhouette of a Min Pin standing on the top of a faraway hill, you would know it was a Min Pin. They are that distinctive.

This kind of dedication says a lot about the people who have fostered and maintained the breed. Like their breed, Min Pin people are unique—and delightful.

For people who are just getting to know the breed, my intention has been to present as much as possible about the joys of owning a Min Pin. In addition, I have not been adverse to relating some of the needs of the breed that might or might not meet and blend with the desires of the prospective owner. Information is the best tool a dog owner can have, and this book presents information about the Min Pin in both breadth and depth.

For people who are already Min Pin owners, there is new information and there is joy in this book. There are stories shared by breeders and trainers that will delight any fancier. There are also sections in the book that will be useful even to experienced breeders regarding litter management, health and first aid. Reference material in the five appendices will be useful and of interest to the breed devotee.

After judging Miniature Pinschers for nearly three decades, rest assured that I have my own opinions and interpretations about their structure and character. That is reflected throughout this book along with my love and admiration of the breed. With that, I deliver to you, the newcomer or the experienced owner, the Miniature Pinscher.

JACKLYN HUNGERLAND, PH.D.
California, 2000

(Photograph by Deckert)

CHAPTER ONE

Is the Miniature Pinscher Right for You?

"Our first Miniature Pinscher was an education to us. We were amazed to discover how big this small dog is."
—MARGARET BAGSHAW

All you have to do is look at a Miniature Pinscher puppy, and you will lose your heart. Most buyers of other breeds are cautioned that their cute little thing might grow up to be a 75-pound "presence" in the household. Not so with the Min Pin. That cute little puppy will remain a small, but tough, little guy. There's nothing "wimpy" about a Min Pin. Because of their diminutive size, you could face a terrible temptation to carry Min Pins around. But these are not necessarily cuddle-bugs, and you might find that your dog doesn't really appreciate this kind of attention.

If a Min Pin is properly socialized and well cared for, he can be a delight to own and will live a long life. Because owning a dog is a long-term commitment, however, your decision must be informed and well thought-out. With advance planning and education, your decision to acquire a Min Pin will be the right one.

You know the size of a Barbie doll—now you know what to expect in the size of a Min Pin. (Photograph by Stamm)

A CANINE OF CONTRASTS

There are lots of small dogs, so why would you want to be owned by a Min Pin? A Min Pin can be as fearless and as tough as any other breed of dog one moment—and the next moment he'll bound into your lap to drown you in kisses. He is a fearless protector, a loyal friend and an entertaining clown who will perform for you for hours. He can warn you of an unwelcome visitor, or he will just lie on your lap on a cold night and keep you warm. He can mesmerize you as he runs around in circles endlessly chasing imaginary rodents in your living room. In other words, the Min Pin is a dog of contrasts.

When placed with the right owner and given the proper training, the Min Pin will become that person's most treasured friend. If the owner cannot provide the gently firm training and attention (and the patience!) required by the dog, a Min Pin can become depressed, unruly and uncontrollable. A Min Pin in the right home can love you with a heart ten times his size; in the wrong home, he can wreak the havoc of a dog ten times his size.

If you work all day and can only look after your dog morning and night, don't get a Min Pin. If you want a super-serious companion, don't get a Min Pin. If you don't think you have the patience to live with a toddler that never grows up, don't get a Min Pin.

On the other hand, you might have what it takes to be a Min Pin person if you want a friend forever, a heating pad, a guardian, a comedian, an acrobat and a buddy that will follow you wherever you lead—and if you're willing to devote your love, respect, time, care, money, thoughts and zeal to a dog that has all of man's qualities and none of his vices.

As you can see, the Min Pin is not a beginner's breed, and it is not a breed for everyone. Miniature Pinschers are inquisitive and have a lot of energy. They need to investigate everything and will go to great lengths to do so, including developing amazing skills in the art of escape.

Rebel Without a Pause . . .

No doubt about it, Miniature Pinschers are dynamite in a small package. Perhaps their zest for life is

After a good run, a group nap provides a quiet hour. (Photograph by Warfield)

best portrayed by a very special Miniature Pinscher: Biker Dolly.

No other breed can claim a dog with the special notoriety attained by Georgette Curran's chocolate-and-rust Min Pin, Biker Dolly. Georgette and her husband are ardent motorcycle enthusiasts. Min Pins being what they are—and Dolly being a definitive Min Pin—the dog couldn't stand to be left behind when her owners would go out biking. Accepting the inevitable, Georgette outfitted Dolly with her own leather jacket, her own helmet and a bag in which she rides the road.

Can you picture that? Well, thousands of people did as Biker Dolly won second place on the television show *America's Funniest Home Videos*. Many are

convinced that if Dolly could actually drive her own bike, she would be long gone on her own biking adventures.

. . . Or "Innocent" Angel?

If things are not going their way, Min Pins can be inventive and clever. A successful breeder shares this story:

I was ready to go to church and couldn't find my car keys. I had to stay home from church, as this was the only set of keys I had. I searched the house the entire day and never did find the keys. I emptied my purse five times, looked in the closets, the yard, the car—everywhere! I was getting worried because I had to go to work the next day. In the morning when I let my Min Pin out of her crate, I found my keys. They were stashed under her blankets. When I found the keys, there she stood, grinning from ear to ear and acting almost as if she was humble. She knew she had done a bad thing, but her smile just wouldn't let me be mad at her.

EXPLORING THE WORLD OF THE MINIATURE PINSCHER

Before you go looking for puppies, you will need to tap in to all the resources available to you. A reasonable plan follows.

Curl Up with Some Good Books

In addition to the book you have in your hand, numerous materials are available to help you learn

Safety is always a concern for bikers, so Dolly must wear her helmet (designed to cover and protect her ears) and her skid-proof leather jacket. Her fleecy snuggle bag gives her just the right warmth and comfort on the road. (Photograph by Georgette Curran)

about the Miniature Pinscher. Read as many books and articles about the breed as you can. After doing this, you'll know with some certainty whether the Miniature Pinscher is the breed of dog for you. Check this book's bibliography for important reading and video materials; there's no lack of information about the capabilities of the popular Min Pin.

Talk to the Experts

First, if you have access to the Internet, visit the Miniature Pinscher Club of America's Web page, at http://members.aol.com/mpcapec/mpcafaqs.html, for the ultimate in expert information.

If there is a dog show in your area, plan to attend. To get inside information on what it's like to live with a Min Pin, chat with the breeders and exhibitors after the dogs are judged. After the judging, people are a bit more relaxed and are not busy primping their dogs (although there's not too much of that necessary with a Min Pin). It's a good idea to get to the show well ahead of time and to get a schedule of when the breeds are being judged. (If the breeders and their dogs immediately leave the grounds after the judging, you've missed you chance.) If you can find a benched show, where the breeders, exhibitors and their dogs are required to stay at the show all day, be sure to take advantage of this great opportunity for conversations about the breed. But do be aware that benched shows are somewhat rare these days. Of course, you also should be aware that not all Min Pins are show dogs. The dogs you see at a show will look very glamorous.

However, unless you plan to get involved in showing, you will not need a "perfect" dog. Most breeders are happy to find good homes for their pet-quality puppies or their retired show dogs and brood bitches. In fact, these older dogs often make the best pets. So, even if your Min Pins plans involve companion-only activities, be sure to discuss them with experienced breeders.

If you're not able to get to a dog show (or even if you are), make use of the reference sources in

Appendix A, "Organizations and More Information."

FACING OFF WITH FACT AND FICTION

After you've read all the information you can acquire and have talked to breeders and lovers of the breed, be sure that you and anyone else who will be involved with your Min Pin have a clear picture of what to expect.

There is a certain spirituality among bikers, and Dolly seems to have it! One caution: Don't try this at home. (Photograph by Georgette Curran)

Min Pin Misconceptions

I usually like to start a discussion with the pros rather than the cons, but this is one situation where common misbeliefs should be dispelled from the beginning.

Miniature Pinscher ≠ Little Doberman

Even though they may look like it, Min Pins are *not* miniature-sized versions of the Doberman Pinscher. The Min Pin is a much older breed than the Doberman. In fact, Herr Doberman (the developer of that breed) wanted to breed a larger and heavier version of the small but fierce little Miniature Pinscher. If you really want a little Doberman, don't bring home a Min Pin.

Toy Dog ≠ Toy

Yes, the Min Pin *is* a Toy breed, but it is not a child's toy. This dog is probably too active for young children. Min Pins can be wriggly, and even an adult might have trouble holding one—a fall can mean broken bones, so handing a Min Pin to a young child is a risky idea. However, older children who are trained in interacting with dogs are probably good prospects for owning a Miniature Pinscher. Moreover, Min Pins will adore children if they are raised around children who treat them gently and are taught responsibility. Likewise, if children are allowed to grab them, hit them or treat them roughly, Min Pins will quickly learn to run from a child. Once hurt, a Min Pin never forgets. This necessity for gentle interaction applies to adult dogs as well as puppies—even an adult Min Pin can easily be injured by rough handling.

Don't chase a Min Pin, either. If the dog is chased and snatched up quickly, he will be frightened and might develop lifelong behavioral problems, such as snapping at hands or running away whenever someone attempts to pick him up. Even though he thinks he's tough, the Min Pin is a small dog and must be treated accordingly. He doesn't tolerate the kind of rough-housing one might engage in with a larger dog. Games just have to be on a smaller scale—suited to his size.

Min Pins ≠ Money

Owning one or more Miniature Pinschers is *not* a way to fame and fortune. Breeding should be left to those who are experienced in the problems involved in breeding small dogs. No one—I repeat, *no one*—makes money breeding dogs if it is done ethically and correctly.

It is always best to let the Min Pin approach a child or young person, and this should be done under proper supervision. (Photograph by Westover)

Do not fool yourself into thinking that you will have litters of puppies. A surplus of discarded Min Pins certainly is not needed. Every dog should have its own proper lifelong home. This is why most reputable breeders sell their pets with contracts requiring the pup to be spayed or neutered or on a limited registration, which prohibits offspring of that puppy from being registered. Refer to Chapter 12, "To Breed or Not to Breed," for more in-depth information concerning the challenge of breeding your Min Pin.

Positively Min Pin

Of course, there are lots of endearing qualities to be found in this breed. Although every dog is an individual, many charming characteristics seem to

be universal in the Miniature Pinscher. If you're looking for a little dog with a lot of personality, the Min Pin might be right for you.

The Action-Packed Min Pin

The Min Pin is a very active breed. These dogs are generally healthy and usually live well into their teens. They're also so energetic that some people consider them to be hyperactive—they're always busy, busy, busy, keeping track of everything that is going on in and around the house. They like—and, in fact, need—a lot of exercise to burn off some of this energy. The Miniature Pinscher Club of America claims that living with a Min Pin is "like living with a roomful of toddlers who never grow up."

After a good run, a Min Pin will happily take up your lap for a snooze as you pass your evening hours. Then, if the dog has been brought up properly, he will be happy to sleep in his crate—or with you, whether in, on or around your bed, if you decide that this is okay. The selection is up to you. If you raise your Min Pin from the start sleeping in a crate and using an exercise pen, that becomes his definition of how life will be. If not, you may come to regret it. But let's learn more about the breed—and you.

The Good Little Guardian

Min Pins are small and compact, but they're very muscular dogs. They're fearless, animated, intensely curious and always full of vigor. In fact, the Min Pin thinks he is a very large dog, and he earns his title "King of Toys" just on the basis of attitude alone. These are excellent watchdogs, but they will bark at just about anything, including that dust bunny you missed when vacuuming. Of course, this can be an undesirable trait, but it can be avoided if the dog is trained right from the beginning not to bark at meaningless things.

The Curious Cutie

These dogs have a need to investigate everything and will go to great lengths to do so. They will climb over or dig under a barrier to get to where they *think* they should be, looking into trouble or creating it. A Min Pin owner really must dog-proof the house because these dogs will find every lost contact lens, straight pin, paper clip and other detritus that may have been nestled into your carpet for years. Chances are good that your dog will proceed to eat or inhale these objects, so watch your Min Pin carefully or you will develop a meaningful relationship with your veterinarian.

A Wash-n-Wear Breed

The Miniature Pinscher is a low-maintenance breed, which should appeal to the pet owner. These dogs need only occasional brushing and infrequent bathing. They do need to have their toenails trimmed on a regular basis, but if you

Min Pins have a lot of energy and will keep you on your toes. (Photograph by Mary Bloom)

don't like to do it yourself, you can arrange for services for a small fee at the local groomer's.

The City Sophisticate

With more people living in apartments these days, Min Pins can be the answer to that need for a companion dog. They're relatively easy to train and make good pets for adults living in small quarters. With consistent awareness on your part, you even can train your Min Pin to use a litter box (but this should never substitute entirely for those long walks in pursuit of squirrels and butterflies). Another benefit to dog lovers with limited space is that, because of their small size, Min Pins really don't cost much to feed.

You don't need a large home to have enough room for a Min Pin. (Photograph by Mary Bloom)

The only problem that might develop, as noted previously, is excessive barking. Interestingly enough, one remedy for the overly busy barker is to get another Min Pin. Two dogs often keep each other amused and comforted.

WHO ELSE HAS BEEN "PINNED"?

Over the years, many famous people have been owned by Miniature Pinschers. As a small breed, Min Pins make excellent travel companions for people who are on the road most of the time. These dogs fit easily under the seat of an airplane and are welcome at most motels, especially if they sleep in a crate.

Just a few of the people who have been charmed by Min Pins are

- Demi Moore
- Helen Chrysler Green, of the Chrysler dynasty
- Veronica Cooper, Gary Cooper's wife
- Charles "Lucky" Luciano

A Coat Color for Everyone

Different colors appeal to different tastes, and Min Pins are available in colors that will appeal to just about everyone: reds, stag reds, black and rust, chocolate and rust, and blue. The most common color in the breed is red because this color is dominant genetically. Next in abundance come the black-and-rust coat and then the chocolate-and-rust coat. The blue dogs are not allowed to be shown. Even though breeders of blues are devoted to them, coat problems in blue dogs are attributed to a mutant gene that has not yet been eradicated. You'll find examples of the different colors throughout this book, and the different types are featured in Chapter 11, "Headliners."

The color that appeals to you is the one you should pursue. Breeders tend to believe that the color they favor is also the color with the best intelligence and temperament, but overall these traits appear to be level among the different colors.

MIN PIN PRICES

If you have fallen in love with the breed after taking into account all the pros and cons—and this is easy to do—you'll be faced with the dreaded bottom line. Be prepared to pay a tidy sum for your Min Pin. Whether or not you buy for showing, remember that you are making an investment in a long-term companion. If you prorate the purchase amount over the fifteen years or so of your friend's expected life span, you will see that your puppy is relatively inexpensive.

If you can't afford to buy a puppy at the market prices, consider saving an older puppy or adult from the rescue services offered through local Min Pin breed clubs or through the national "Parent Club," the Miniature Pinscher Club of America. Whatever you do, if you have any doubts at all, contact the MPCA through the resources included in Appendix A.

Regardless of what your new companion costs, you're in for a lot of fun. You will be entertained, frustrated, and very, very humbled by your new friend. A few tips: Stay in close contact with the breeder from whom you got your puppy. Check on training classes that may be offered in your area, and prepare yourself for a challenge and a laugh or two. Whether you have selected a show or a pet Miniature Pinscher, remember that this is a breed that will need your devotion to become your best friend.

The Miniature Pinscher is known as "King of Toys," and he's perfectly comfortable with that title. (Photograph by Mary Bloom)

CHAPTER TWO

The Miniature Pinscher Heritage

"The best dogs of any breed have always been bred by those who truly love them . . .
an ideal in the heart and mind's eye of one person."

—VIVA LEONE RICKETTS

The Miniature Pinscher is a human-made breed that was developed for appeal as a small, easily maintained companion dog. From beginning versions of the breed to present-day standards, the Min Pin has been a useful addition to home and hearth. How the breed as we know it today developed might help you understand why the breed is active, inquisitive and charming, as well as why it is useful.

A BREED OF ITS OWN

Many people think that the Miniature Pinscher is just a smaller version of the Doberman Pinscher. In fact, the Min Pin a much older breed than the Doberman. Some fanciers argue that the Min Pin was bred down from the German Pinscher, a dog smaller than the Doberman but much larger than the

Min Pin. However, most students of the dog believe that the Min Pin and the German Pinscher evolved at about the same time via different paths.

The Pinscher-type breeds are similar, but they are *not* small Doberman Pinschers—in fact, it is the other way around. Dobermans are much larger and were developed by Herr Doberman in Germany, with the first distinct member of the breed appearing about 1890. Herr Doberman's goal was to breed a giant dog that would look like the small ancestor of the Min Pin, so the Doberman actually is a larger version of the Min Pin.

The Miniature Pinscher is decidedly a breed apart. It is smaller and more affable than the German Pinscher and, as a Toy breed, is more easily adapted to apartment or smaller home living.

The German Pinscher is a medium-sized dog that stands about 16 to 19 inches tall and weighs between 25 and 35 pounds. He has been called the Medium, the Standard or just Pinscher. (Photograph by Rubin)

HOW DID THE MIN PIN DEVELOP?

Dogs thought to be Min Pins have been pictured by the old masters for several hundred years, but no written record of the breed can be found until 1836. At that time, German Dr. H.G.

Reichernbach, a geneticist and devoted Min Pin enthusiast, stated that the breed was most likely a cross between the Dachshund and the Italian Greyhound (although he also speculated that some of the Pug breed might have been involved). The Min Pin's long, graceful legs could well have been inherited from the Italian Greyhound, and its coat could certainly have come from the smooth Dachshund.

In Reichernbach's time, the breed was known as the Reh Pinscher because of its resemblance to the small, red deer found in the forests of Germany. A working-class dog of the Reh Pinscher weighed 18 to 25 pounds, but the Toys, which ranged from 2½ to 5 pounds, became more popular due to their smaller size, which suited them to the home more than the barn.

Around 1883, the breed was registered in Germany, and more careful documentation of the breed began. The German Pinscher Club, which included all forms of Pinschers, was organized in 1895. At that time, the Reh Pinscher was not a highly popular dog because it was coarse in appearance and came in various sizes and colors. The dog preferred to be in the stables hunting

*The dog pictured here is thought by experts to be the Reh
Pinscher, or more likely the Min Pin, on his pillow.
(Photograph courtesy Secord Gallery)*

vermin, and it had a difficult time adapting to the
sedentary life in the homes of its owners. Fanciers
of parlor dogs wanted an amenable, toy-sized dog,
but the Reh Pinscher wanted to be outside working. In general form and occasional coloration, the
Reh Pinscher showed a similarity to the English
Black-and-Tan Terrier (known as the Manchester
Terrier in the United States), so the Reh Pinscher
was classified into the Terrier family.

To reap the economic benefits, breeders turned
their focus toward producing smaller dogs that
would meet household requirements. In this intermediate stage of its development, the Min Pin
bore a remarkable resemblance to the Italian
Greyhound, which was very likely used to bring
the Pinscher size down and to introduce a more
compliant temperament into the breed. This similarity has diminished as the Min Pin has developed
into a mature breed.

Around the turn of the century, the breed
went through a decline in quality. Because the
breeders were paying so much attention to gener-
ating small dogs, they neglected to breed for stamina, and the dogs generally became less healthy
and less vigorous. In addition, as fad would have it,
the red dogs lost favor to the black-and-rust dogs.
As we know today, red is the dominant color in
this breed, and black-and-rust is a recessive color.
Unfortunately, dogs with recessive color genes
were bred together more often. This furthered the
decline in the dogs' stamina and health. Recessive-
gene breeding also produced harlequin and
brindle-patterned Reh Pinschers, to satisfy some
people's desire for exotic-looking dogs.

Finally, by 1914, breeders began to pay more
attention to the body, temperament and soundness
of the breed. Soon reds became more popular and
were of good quality, type and color. Even though
more recessive colors emerged—notably blue and
chocolate—the breed became healthy, powerful
and of good character, all conditions demanded by
their German fanciers. In lean times, the Min Pin
proved to the Germans to be a self-sufficient dog.
With its hunting instinct, the Min Pin killed rats
and vermin in the barns and homes of its owners,
not only ridding people of these disease-ridden
menaces but also feeding itself. Thus, at no expense
to the household, an efficient exterminator was in
residence at all times.

During and just after World War I, the German breeders needed money and sold many dogs of poor quality to the Swiss. These dogs were reported as stunted, nervous little dogs with poor coats and frail little legs. Breed quality decreased, and about 1918 the Reh Pinscher Klub joined with the Schnauzer Klub to rescue the Schnauzer, the Smooth-Haired Pinscher and the Reh Pinscher. The Klub took pains to develop standards for the breeds that specified the nature and character of the dogs. With deliberate breeding they became alert, watchful and keen, and they acquired an inquisitive approach to strangers and strange situations.

The best specimens of Reh Pinschers were exported in large numbers into the United States by breeders in the Netherlands who had combined their stock with that of the breeders in Germany. That cooperative breeding effort resulted in a period of excellence for the breed.

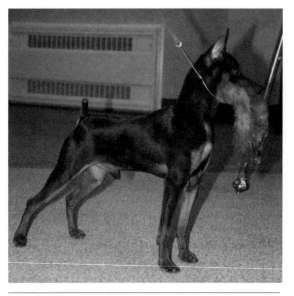

The "hunter" is still alive in the Min Pin, even if the prey is a toy. (Photograph by Warfield)

THE MINIATURE PINSCHER COMES TO AMERICA

Prior to 1928, few Min Pins were found in the United States, although people were becoming aware of the breed and an enthusiastic swell was taking place in the breed's favor. The dog's bearing and its "big heart in a small package" earned it the very honorable title of "King of Toys." The Min Pin retains this title today. Brought out of the barn, the Min Pin soon became appreciated as a family pet. It proved to be an excellent watchdog and companion, and its easy care and alertness added to its desirability.

In 1925, a black-and-rust bitch, Asta von Sandreuth, became the first Min Pin registered with the American Kennel Club (AKC) under the breed name Pinscher (Toy), which was listed in the Miscellaneous Class and shown under the German standard. In these early years, prominent dog fancier Mrs. Henrietta Proctor Donnell became enamored of the Min Pin and imported several directly from Germany. These dogs were exciting additions to her Etty Haven kennels. Most prominent was the red Ch. Konig Hanzelmannchen, a celebrated sire and outstanding winner. Shortly after arriving in the United States, this dog made his debut at the Westminster show in 1931, where he was awarded Reserve Winners. As soon as he became acclimated, he began to win on a regular basis. He was named Best of Breed at Westminster

WHY IS IT CALLED A "PINSCHER"?

Some confusion surrounds the origins of the name "Pinscher." The exact translation from German is "to pinsch," and this is followed by the same English interpretation. If you understand that a terrier—or "ratter," which the Pinscher was in his barn days—kills its prey by pinching the spinal cord at the back of the neck, the meaning of this term becomes clearer. This is done very swiftly, and the neck is broken. Most terrier breeds are *required* to have complete incisors in their dentition because those teeth are used to "pinch" and kill their prey.

A remnant of this ancient instinct exists in the Miniature Pinscher of today. He likes to pinch every inch of his toys, and he will nip or pinch as a warning to other dogs that are too friendly. Sometimes he will even pinch at his owner to get attention, or just in play. Incidentally, this is a characteristic common in the Italian Greyhound as well, and it is said that this is an additional sign that the Italian Greyhound was indeed a part of the development of the Min Pin.

"Rat terriers" tended to live side by side in the barns of Europe, as evidenced by this painting of two seemingly compatible terriers. Note, however, that one of the dogs happens to be a black-and-rust Miniature Pinscher. (Photograph courtesy of Secord Gallery)

In the case of the Min Pin's name, instead of form following function, it is a matter of *name* following function, as "miniature" is the operative description of the breed.

---

in 1932, 1934, 1937 and 1938. In 1934, he was named the top Miniature Pinscher at the prestigious Morris and Essex show sponsored by Mrs. Geraldine (Rockefeller) Dodge. Etty Haven also presented the Best in Show team of Min Pins at the Westminster shows of 1937, 1938 and 1941.

The Miniature Pinscher Club of America (MPCA), was formed in 1929 by fanciers who were devoted to promoting this small but mighty dog into recognition by the American Kennel Club (AKC). At first the breed was classified in the Terrier Group because of its background and its terrier-like attitude. However, the MPCA's position prevailed, and one year later the breed was reclassified by the AKC into the Toy Group with the title of Pinscher (Toy). In 1935, the first standard for the breed was adopted by the MPCA and was approved by the AKC. That standard prevailed until it was revised in 1950 and 1958, and then revamped in 1980 (you'll get more details on the breed standard in Chapter 3, "The Official Breed Standard with Interpretation"). In 1972, the breed was officially named the Miniature Pinscher.

THE RISE IN THE MIN PIN'S POPULARITY

A good gauge of the popularity of a breed is based on the number of dogs of that breed registered by the American Kennel Club. For example, in 1941 only 24 Miniature Pinschers were registered. After World War II, the numbers increased, but in 1955 only 170 registrations were recorded, bringing the total number of Min Pins registered at that time to a little more than 800. In 1998, however, 22,675 Min Pin registrations were recorded, showing enormous growth between 1955 and 1998. In that year, the Min Pin was rated sixteenth in popularity of all breeds registered by the AKC in the United States.

Kennels That Contributed to the Breed's Strength

The development of any breed depends upon dedicated breeders, those who sacrifice personal time and immeasurable effort to work constantly for the betterment of the breed. The history of the Min Pin would not be complete without mentioning some of the dogs and kennels that formed the recent history of the breed and made it what it is today. Through their tireless effort and search for perfection, many breeders have contributed to the breed. Although it is hard to select just a few, there is never space to discuss or present them all.

Mill Mass

The first of the great Min Pins was probably Mrs. Mildred Mastin's Ch. Patzie Von Mill Mass. Patzie came on the heels of many fine specimens, but she is the first to stand out as a great dog that was recognized by all Min Pin enthusiasts and the dog fancy in general. In the early 1950s, Patzie made her mark with some twenty all-breed Best in Show awards. Ch. Patzie Von Mill Mass displays all the elements of breed type that are vital to the breed: a strong topline; a chiseled and refined head;

Ch. Patzie Von Mill. (Photograph by Ludwig)

a long, arched neck and feet that could stand on a dime. She was the first of a chain of great Min Pins that would have a meaningful influence on the look of the breed in the United States.

Bel-Roc

During the mid–1950s, Mrs. Mary (Booher) Summers came into the limelight when her kennel produced Ch. Bel-Roc's Dobe V. Enztal, one of the most celebrated black-and-rust Min Pins in the history of the breed. The further importance of Dobe is his contribution to the pedigree of the famous dogs of the Rebel-Roc kennels.

Rebel-Roc

Mr. E.W. "Tip" Tipton was the breeder of the Rebel-Roc Min Pins, the most famous of which was Ch. Rebel-Roc's Casanova Von Kurt, better known as Little Daddy.

Little Daddy was the first of the great sires, and he is the Min Pin that was chosen to represent the breed on the logo of the MPCA. His picture has been used more than that of any other dog to represent the ideal of the breed.

Little Daddy is acknowledged as probably the greatest Min Pin ever and is considered to be one of the fathers, if not *the* father, of the modern Min

One of Dobe's outstanding kennel mates was Ch. Bel-Roc's Sugar Von Enztal, National Specialty winner in 1958. (Photograph by Shafer)

Ch. Rebel-Roc's Casanova Von Kurt ("Little Daddy").

Pin. He won seventy-five Best in Show titles (the first one at 8 months of age) and sired forty-seven Champions.

Bo-Mar

At about the same time that Mr. Tipton was breeding Min Pins, Dr. Buris Boshell founded the celebrated Bo-Mar line. His kennel was based on the dogs of Bel-Roc and Rebel-Roc. Many prestigious Min Pins carried the Bo-Mar banner, chief among them the outstanding Ch. Bo-Mar's Roadrunner, who sired some seventy-three Champions and made a major contribution to the general look of the breed today.

Also of note was Ch. Bo-Mar's Drummer Boy, the first top winning black-and-rust dog.

Drummer Boy paved the way for such subsequent black-and-rust winners as Ch. K-Roc's

Black Doubloon, Best of Breed at the National Specialty in 1973; and Ch. Talana's Sky Man of Haiko, the first Miniature Pinscher Champion to finish a championship in Hawaii.

Sanbrook

If ever one lady deserves to be called the matriarch of the modern Miniature Pinscher, it is Ann Dutton of Sanbrook fame. More than 100 Min Pin Champions proudly carry the Sanbrook prefix, more than any other kennel in the breed's history.

Today the Sanbrook kennel continues to produce exemplary dogs through Ch. Sanbrook Ready Set Go and Ch. Sanbrook Twist and Shout.

Ch. Bo-Mar's Roadrunner.

Ch. Bo-Mar's Drummer Boy. (Photograph courtesy of MPCA)

Among Sanbrook's outstanding winners was Ch. Sanbrook Silk Electric, a three-time National Specialty winner and producer of more than seventy Champions. (Photograph by Ashbey Photography)

Jay-Mac's Impossible Dream ("Impy"). (Photograph by Cain Photography)

Jay-Mac

One of the most memorable Min Pins was the bitch, Ch. Jay-Mac's Impossible Dream.

"Impy," as she was known, was indeed an impossible dream for her breeder, Johnny

MacNamara. In the early 1970s, Impy was the quintessential elegant Min Pin. She stepped into a ring and demanded attention. She was a show dog without equal, with more than seventy-five Best in Show wins. Following her type, the breed would ever after be an elegant one without a trace of the cobby rat-chasing dog in the barns during previous centuries.

Ch. Carlee Nubby Silk. (Photograph courtesy of MPCA)

The 1998 National Specialty winner, Ch. Whitehouse's Hot Damm Here I Am, shown with judge Anne Rogers Clark. (Photograph by Glasbrook)

In addition to Impy, the Jay-Mac banner was carried by Hall of Fame sires such as Ch. Jay-Mac's Moon Eagle, Ch. Jay-Mac's Pat Hand and Ch. Jay-Mac's Pippin, all of whom injected newfound style and elegance into the breed's gene pool. Pat Hand was a grandson of the famous Little Daddy, was a Best in Show and Best in Specialty Show winner, and also was the winner of the National Specialty in 1974, so it is easy to see how quality begets quality.

Jay-Mac bitches were the distinguished dams in Min Pin history. Ch. Jay-Mac's Silk Stockings produced an outstanding twenty-five Champions. Impy's dam, Ch. Jay-Mac's Rambling Rose, was the dam of twenty-two Champions.

Together, Silk Stockings and Rambling Rose produced more Champions than any other bitches in the history of the breed. As a consequence, many great Min Pins of today have "Jay-Mac" in their pedigrees, and "Jay-Mac" has become an adjective to describe any Min Pin that has elegance and style.

Sunsprite

Sunsprite is the bannerhead of Marcia Tucker. Although her kennel produced many fine Min Pins, the top producer in the breed, Ch. Carlee Nubby Silk, was a Sunsprite dog but was not bred there. He was chosen by the breeder to enhance the breed, and that is exactly what he did.

Ch. Carlee Nubby Silk is credited with siring 117 Champions, more than any other Min Pin.

Bred by Carol Garrison and Ann Dutton, Nubby holds a record that will be a challenge to break, and he is an example of the mark one spectacular producer can leave on a breed.

Whitehouse

Consistently in the limelight have been the Whitehouse kennel's dogs of breeder Judith White. Ch. Whitehouse's Hot Damm Here I Am, was the first black-and-rust Min Pin to win the National Specialty since 1981.

MAINTAINING THE UNIQUE QUALITIES OF THE MINIATURE PINSCHER

The Min Pin has been saved from the potential devastation that comes with overpopularity of a breed. No movies or television programs have featured the Min Pin, which has saved the breed from being "discovered" by the general buying public of the United States. That's a blessing, because the Min Pin is not for every household. Being a hidden treasure helps preserve the breed from overbreeding, which often results in filling shelters with rejected dogs. Instead, breeders can focus on maintaining or improving the quality of the breed.

CHAPTER THREE

The Official Breed Standard with Interpretation

"I feel very safe with my Min Pin and know that she would protect me to the very best of her abilities, and that's not something that can be taught."

—JANICE ARNOLD

As mentioned in Chapter 1, "Is the Miniature Pinscher Right for You?," the Miniature Pinscher is *not* a bred-down Doberman. What, then, is this dog? How is it supposed to look? What is the breed's character? This chapter discusses both of these topics in connection with the breed standard, a description of the "ideal" Miniature Pinscher.

Unlike many breeds, there is no apparent difference between a show dog and a good-quality pet in a Min Pin. No special trims make one look different from the other. A show dog's personality, its temperament and its health should be no different from that of a pet-quality Min Pin.

The dogs chosen for showing must adhere as closely as possible to the standard for the breed because they are judged against that standard. While it is nice if your pet Min Pin is also of show quality, this is certainly not required. Nonetheless, the breed character is one of the most attractive aspects of the dog,

Ch. Dynasty's Jackie's Surprise gives you a good idea of what you should expect to see when you look at a Min Pin with lots of breed character. (Photograph by Alex Smith)

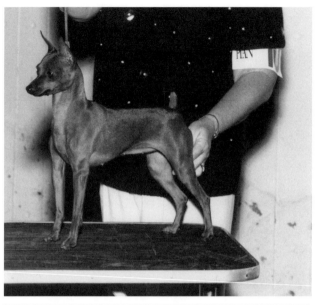

Ch. Talana's Diamonds 'N' Sable poses in the show ring while winning honors. But Diamonds 'N' Sable isn't just a great show dog—she's also a beloved household companion! (Photograph by Callea)

and owners will want a dog that possesses most of the essence of that character.

THE EVOLUTION OF THE STANDARD FOR THE MINIATURE PINSCHER

Every recognized breed has a breed standard that specifies the way a breed should look and act. The standard's purpose is to help maintain some consistency in the breed and is a document for judges to use in evaluating the breeding quality of individual dogs. The standard is also a set of goals for breeders to set in planning and forming their breeding programs. The careful buyer looking for a good Miniature Pinscher will use the breed standard as an educational tool and for reference in the decision-making involved in a purchase.

The breed standard in use in the United States was written by the Miniature Pinscher Club of America and was approved by the American Kennel Club in 1980. This standard was reformatted in 1990 without changes to its content or

---

specifications. The same basic standard is in use under United Kennel Club (UKC) and Federacion Canine Internationale (FCI) Rules. In the United Kingdom (UK), the standard allows for the color blue in addition to the colors and combinations customary in the United States. The FCI and UK standards also have a height specification of 10 to 12 inches, which differs from the AKC specification of 10 to 12 ½ inches at the withers. For an excellent comparison of these three breed standards, see Sari Brewster Tietjen's book *The New Miniature Pinscher* (Howell Book House, 1988).

In its Judges' Study Group presentation, the MPCA includes a comparison of the breed standards that were in place in 1929, 1935, 1950, 1958 and 1980. These comparisons are interesting because of major changes that occurred on the path to creating the breed standard of 1980. While these standards agree that the desired size for the Min Pin should be about 11 or 11 ½ inches at the withers, the degree to which variations in that size—both under and over—will be tolerated differ. Until 1958, a specification of weight as well as height was included in the standard, but weight no longer is used as a criterion.

Perhaps the two areas of greatest conflict over these seventy years were the definition of a "hackney-like" gait and the list of admissible colors. The next sections explore these issues in more detail.

The Min Pin's Hackney-Like Gait

The 1935 standard referred to the dog's gait as "similar to that of a good hackney pony." This

A hackney pony struts its stuff. (Illustration by Karl Brandt)

transformed in the 1950 standard into a "precise hackney gait." In 1980 and in the current standard, the gait reverted to "hackney-like action." What does "hackney-like" mean?

A hackney pony walks in a very showy manner, with a lot of high-stepping action in front and very little push from the rear quarters. The distinctive front action is a high lift of the front leg with a visible "break" at the wrist—the pastern and hoof drop down to become nearly perpendicular to the ground. This action has very little reach forward. Notice that the lift for the foreleg originates at the elbow, which is not a strong movement. Notice also that the hind leg lifts more upward than forward, allowing for very little drive from the hindquarters. This combination of little push from the hindquarters and little reach forward demonstrates that the hackney pony is not a racehorse; he does not cover very much ground, and what he does cover is done at a slow and studied pace.

The Min Pin is flashy and stylish and is similar to the hackney pony in front action, but with more forward reach and more strength in the hindquarters. We'll discuss the dog's movement in more detail later in this chapter.

The physical attributes illustrated by the accompanying photographs allow the Min Pin to cover more ground when it moves than the hackney pony does.

Color Specifications

Some of the original Min Pins had long coats and were various shades of gray. (Many believe that this type of coat resulted from early breeding with the Miniature Schnauzer.) Consequently, until 1980, acceptable colors included solid yellow and blue or blue-toned.

Notice how the proper lift of the Min Pin's front leg comes from the shoulder of the dog, which lends strength to the entire front leg.

The rear leg lifts slightly upward but also forward, allowing the hindquarters to dig in and push with good drive forward.

Until 1935, a Harlequin-like pattern of white with flecks of mostly gray in the body was accepted. Today, these colors are cause for disqualification from breed competition, and the standard sets very specific requirements for color and markings.

THE OFFICIAL BREED STANDARD

The official AKC breed standard (printed in Roman type, with annotations by the author in italics) follows. An abbreviated standard with illustrations is available from the Miniature Pinscher Club of America (see Appendix A, "Organizations and More Information").

GENERAL APPEARANCE— The Miniature Pinscher is structurally a well balanced, sturdy, compact, short-coupled, smooth-coated dog. He naturally is well groomed, proud, vigorous and alert. Characteristic traits are his hackney-like action, fearless animation, complete self-possession, and his spirited presence.

This paragraph gives the reader the overall picture of the Miniature Pinscher and provides a mental image of what to expect in a first impression of the breed.

TEMPERAMENT—Fearless animation, complete self-possession, and spirited presence.

Combined with the previous paragraph of the standard, this description tells the full story of the Miniature Pinscher and the essence of the breed character. A story about the famous Ch. Carlee Nubby Silk, shared by breeder Barbara Stamm, explains temperament very well:

In the early '80s, when Marcia Tucker came to visit, she had Nubby Silk with her. He was to be shown as a Veteran, but he was in glorious condition and was just a clown. We were all talking and laughing around the table when all of a sudden this flash of red dog leaped by me and landed squarely in the middle of the table. It was Nubby, who promptly sat down in the middle of the table and looked around at all of us as if to say, "You are ignoring me, don't you people realize who I am?" Of course, he received the attention he was after and was very pleased with himself.

This rare photo of Margaret Bagshaw with her earliest Min Pins shows the closeness that develops between a Min Pin and his person. (Photograph courtesy of B.J. Shuler)

The Min Pin Attitude

The official breed standard represents the ideal Min Pin, the one that is closest to perfect. That perfection has never been achieved in any breed, even though there are strong contenders among Min Pins. In addition to physical superiority, an important part of breed character is personality, including attitude. If you live with a Min Pin, you will soon realize that you will never be the center of attention again—you will be upstaged by a small dog. There is no doubt that these dogs do believe that they are the King of Toys.

Margaret Bagshaw, maven of the breed, tells how a Min Pin first impressed her. Then a breeder

This red puppy is determined to get to the other side of his baby gate—and if he gets there, he will be gone.

This Min Pin is shown in one of his favorite places: curled up with the pillows on the family room sofa. (Photograph by Mary Bloom)

of Great Danes, Bagshaw was at a dog show where she witnessed a prominent Min Pin leap from his handler's arms to attack a Chow Chow. The size and nature of the Chow did not intimidate the Min Pin one bit. That Min Pin, Ch. King Eric v Konigsbach, went on to win Best in Show that day and later joined the Bagshaws' prominent Canyon Crest kennel.

The Min Pin is an active little dog, gay and cheerful. He jumps and runs about with quick, playful movements. He has a zest for life second to none. He is clean and neat, and he requires very little grooming. The breed also is fearless, which can get a dog into trouble if he's challenging a larger, aggressive dog. A Min Pin *can* get along in your home with larger dogs, but the Min Pin will

CUDDLING UP

You'll find that Min Pins like to snuggle under covers and that they'll burrow in their blankets at night—even in warm weather. Arguably, this behavior is just part of the cuteness of the Min Pin. More likely, however, it represents the fact that Min Pins simply do not tolerate extremes in temperature. In cold weather, they cannot be left out for any length of time because their legs will freeze easily. If you see your Min Pin out in the cold and he appears to be unable to move, go and get him immediately because his legs may be frozen and will not let him move.

want to be king. One breeder tells of having five Min Pins and one Rottweiler living together amiably. However, this is not recommended for the novice owner, as proper training must take place to ensure peace and harmony.

Min Pins will usually bond with one person, but they will love home and family. They are not an outdoor breed and must never be left out as a yard dog. In fact, a secure yard is a must because they tend to climb over or dig under to satisfy their curiosity and their need to see what's happening on the other side of that fence!

Most losses of Min Pins occur when they escape through a tiny opening in a fence or door and are hit by a car, skate-boarder or bicycle. Min Pins are *fast*, and you must never forget that fact if you want to see your dog live to a ripe old age.

Min Pins can always make you laugh, especially if two are together in the household. These dogs love to be the center of attention and so will be very inventive in amusing you. They are very self-important, and some breeders think of them as being conceited. Min Pins may have earned a right to conceit, however, because they are very clever dogs. One breeder who used to travel in her job tells of taking her Min Pin with her on the road. At each hotel, the dog would sit before, during and after the elevator ride, and then would "track" to her room. One time the breeder got off the elevator, but the dog would not budge. He insisted that she had stopped at the wrong floor—and he was right!

Looks alone do not define breed character in the Min Pin, as evidenced by this story from breeder Barbara Stamm:

I had a tiny, tiny bitch that I was sure would never reach 8 inches. I kept her until she was about 5 months old and then sold her to a woman who was a night jailer in some out-of-the-way town in Alaska. This puppy was a holy terror although she looked like a China doll. The woman phoned me about a half hour after she got home from the airport. The puppy had walked out of her crate, looked around and proceeded to tree her 18-pound cat. That is a Min Pin.

General Impressions Applied in the Show Ring

All the manifestations of appearance and character comprise the mental picture that a dog show judge bears in mind when first looking at a class of Min Pins in the show ring. This first impression is important in helping the judge assess the overall quality of a class and that of the individual dogs being judged.

The Min Pin is rarely, if ever, touched by his handler when he is showing; he stands naturally on the floor. However, he may not stand perfectly still for examination by the judge or for photographs, which are usually done on a table.

In fact, because he wants to be in charge of all activities, the Min Pin is usually antsy during the table examination, which includes checking the teeth, eye color, coat color and any disqualifying

Demonstrating an example of what is expected in a good, freestanding presentation in the show ring is Ch. March-On Johnny Ringo, shown here as a puppy but standing tall with adult attitude. (Photograph by E. Michel and Rick Johnson)

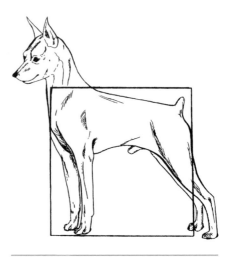

The dimensions indicated in this drawing from the MPCA Illustrated Standard *give a sense of the kind of proportion (balance of height to length) that is desirable.*

characteristics, whether they are breed-specific disqualifications or those covered by the AKC rules.

After the table examination, the dog is moved so that the judge can assess physical soundness, attitude and temperament, and the degree to which the dog meets the prescribed gait.

A more specific and detailed description of the points in the breed that are fully evaluated in the examination are contained in the following sections of the standard.

SIZE, PROPORTION, SUBSTANCE—Size: 10 inches to 12 1/2 inches in height allowed, with desired height 11 inches to 11 1/2 inches measured at highest point of the shoulder blades. Disqualification: Under 10 inches or over 12 1/2 inches in height. Length of males equals height at withers. Females may be slightly longer.

The height specifications are quite clear. Because there is a wide range of permitted size, all dogs within acceptable limits are to be considered equally. In the show ring, any dog measured to be under 10 inches or over 12 1/2 inches in height is to be disqualified. It is the judge's responsibility to use the AKC-approved measuring device, called a wicket, to measure any dog he believes to be outside the allowed limits. He must also measure any dog whose size is questioned by another exhibitor in the ring. Under current AKC rules, three such disqualifications bar the dog for life from further competition. The height is measured at the withers, the highest point of the shoulder blades.

The length referred to is the length of body of the dog as measured from the forechest to the back of the rump. This type of measurement is done just by the judge's eye— no formal measurement or measuring device exists for this.

Proportion, or balance, is just as important as height. It is possible for a dog to be 10 inches tall but to be too refined in bone or too long in body in relation to the length of its legs. Similarly, a 12-inch dog might have very heavy bone and body, or a dog with a very refined bone might have a shallow, "racy" body. None of these would present a picture of proper breed character.

HEAD—In correct proportion to the body. Tapering, narrow with well-fitted but not too prominent foreface which balances with the skull. No indication of coarseness. Eyes

Light or yellow eye color is incorrect and is very undesirable in a Min Pin of any coat color. These lighter eyes tend to give a fierce or terrier-like expression, which is not in character for the breed, even though the dogs are visually alert. (Photograph by Stamm)

full, slightly oval, clear, bright and dark even to a true black, including eye rims, with the exception of chocolates, whose eye rims should be self-colored. Ears set high *[on the skull]*, standing erect from base to tip. May be cropped or uncropped.

Skull appears flat, tapering forward toward the muzzle. Muzzle strong rather than fine and delicate, and in proportion to the head as a whole. Head well balanced with only a slight drop to the muzzle, which is parallel to the top of the skull. Nose black only, with the exception of chocolates, which should have a self-colored nose. Lips and cheeks small, taut and closely adherent to each other. Teeth meet in a scissors bite.

The head of the Miniature Pinscher is one of its distinguishing characteristics. Unfortunately, the standard leaves many areas open to wide ranges of interpretation. For example, it does not dictate the width of skull related to the width and depth of the muzzle. Nor does it give any indication of the length of the skull or the length of the muzzle, or the relationship between these two dimensions. These omissions are the greatest failing of the standard. As a result, breeders, exhibitors and judges have no true guidance as to the correct make and shape of the head.

Two distinct types of head have resulted: the "old-fashioned" head and the "Doberman-type" head. An

A very refined red bitch with a refined, Doberman-like head. (Photograph by Stamm)

old-fashioned head has a broader skull, with nicely chiseled cheeks, a muzzle approximately equal to the skull (from the brow to the rearmost point of the skull, the occiput) and the muzzle somewhat refined and tapering to the nose. The Doberman-type head is a narrower and longer skull, with the same longer muzzle. This type of head has less "stop," or demarcation, between the skull and the muzzle and is more refined. As a result, the dog's head looks more like a Doberman Pinscher's than a Min Pin's.

With the development of two different head types, at least two different body types have emerged and will be noted later.

Ears must always stand erect, whether or not they are cropped.

A red pup with natural, uncropped ears shows a good ear set on the head and correct, upright, erect carriage of the ears. (Photograph by Stamm)

Cropping the ears can affect the dog's expression and can also be used to give the impression of better balance between the head and the body. Sometimes the ears are cropped if the natural ears fail to stand erect or if the ear set on the skull is less than desirable. Remember, though, that a cropped ear is man-made, and a dog with a failed crop is still a Min Pin and can be considered for breeding or placement as a family pet.

NECK, TOPLINE, BODY—
Neck proportioned to head and body, slightly arched, gracefully curved, blending into the shoulders, muscular and free from suggestion of dewlap or throatiness. Topline: Back level or slightly sloping toward the rear, both when standing and gaiting.

Body compact, slightly wedge-shaped, muscular. Forechest well developed. Well-sprung ribs *[ribs that form a rounded arc from the spine downward to the chest below]*. Depth of brisket *[the chest]*, the base line of which is level with points of the elbows. Belly moderately tucked up to denote grace of structural form. Short and strong in loin *[the area between the last rib and the hip bones]*. Croup *[the area between the top of the hip bones and the base of the tail]* level with topline. Tail set high, held erect, docked in proportion to size of dog.

When the standard specifies that the neck should blend into the shoulders, it means that there should be a gentle flow from the back of the neck through its attachment just in front of the shoulder blades and onward to the

The neck should form a strong pedestal to support the head, which should be carried high so that there is a somewhat arrogant appearance attributed to the dog.

back. No rolls of fat should be present at this juncture, and the neck should not look as though it is creating a 90° angle with the back. The front of the neck should have no loose-hanging skin (a dewlap or throatiness), and the throat itself should not be thick and coarse.

The reference to a slightly wedge-shaped body means as viewed from the top, or looking down from above onto the top of the dog. This means that the body tapers somewhat from the rib cage to the rear end of the dog.

FOREQUARTERS—Shoulders clean and sloping with moderate angulation coordinated to permit the hackney-like action. Elbows close to the body. Legs: Strong bone development and small, clean joints. As viewed from the front, straight and upstanding. Pasterns *[the area from the foot pads up to the "wrist" joint]* strong, perpendicular. Dewclaws *[extra, unused nails that usually occur on the lower portion of the front legs]* should be removed. Feet small, catlike, toes strong, well arched and closely knit with deep pads. Nails thick, blunt.

To have proper support for the Min Pin's hackney-like action, which initiates with the shoulder, the shoulder must meet the upper arm with a moderate angle.

The hackney-like action is a strongly controlled series of movements. Without this control coming from strong shoulders, the front legs are inclined to wave around in the air seemingly without direction. This results in what is called the "egg beater" action. "High-stepping" action means that the foreleg lifts—elbow to forefoot—higher than other dogs, whose forward action lies closer to the ground. It does not mean that the front legs are thrown up to approach chin level. Correct lift brings the foreleg approximately level with—or seeming to be an extension of—the pro-sternum or forechest.

Strong shoulders with a proper angle of connection with the upper arm allow the foreleg to lift from the

shoulder. Weak shoulders with straight upper arms produce a "goose step" movement. When the dog moves with the correct hackney-like action, the front legs must move forward with a reaching motion.

HINDQUARTERS—Well muscled quarters set wide enough apart to fit into a properly balanced body. As viewed from the rear, the legs are straight and parallel. From the side, well angulated. Thighs well muscled. Stifles *[the forwardmost point of the thigh]* well defined *[meaning that there is a nice, smoothly curved appearance]*. Hocks *[the area from the lowest hind-leg joint downward to the foot pad is commonly called the hock, although technically the joint itself is the hock]* short, set well apart. Dewclaws should be removed. Feet small, catlike, toes strong, well arched and closely knit with deep pads. Nails thick, blunt.

This young bitch shows with a smooth blend of muscling on the inside and outside of the hips and thighs, which compares favorably with the standard. (Photograph by Stamm)

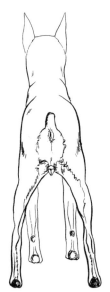

Drawings of the ideal hindquarters from the MPCA Illustrated Standard.

Even though the standard calls for the hindquarters and the thighs to be well-muscled, this does not mean that they will look like a well-developed Bull Terrier or Bulldog. This is a Toy breed, and the Min Pin cannot be so over-burdened with muscle that it looks distended or knotty. Muscling must be smoothly developed and definitely in proportion to the breed's size.

COAT—Smooth, hard and short, straight and lustrous, closely adhering to and uniformly covering the body.

The Miniature Pinscher is a low-maintenance breed. However, exhibitors often succumb to the temptation of trimming more than nails and whiskers. Some dogs are shown with their necks and muzzles shaved, although this is not aesthetically pleasing. It is important that the coat be healthy and sleek.

COLOR—Solid, clear red. Stag red (red with intermingling of black hairs). Black with sharply defined rust-red markings on cheeks, lips, lower jaw, throat, twin spots above eyes and chest, lower half of forelegs, inside of hind legs and vent *[anal]* region, lower portion of hocks and feet. Black pencil stripes on toes. Chocolate with rust-red markings the same as specified for blacks, except brown pencil stripes on toes. In the solid red and stag red, a rich vibrant medium to dark shade is preferred. Disqualifications: Any color other than listed. Thumb mark (patch of black hair surrounded by rust on the front of the foreleg between the foot and the wrist; on chocolates, the patch is chocolate hair). White on any part of dog which exceeds one-half inch in its longest dimension.

The black or chocolate coat with rust-red markings is typical of those in many breeds that are referred to commonly as black-and-tan markings. As a distinction, however, the "tan" markings of the Min Pin are more a rust-red color. It is hard to find the absolutely correct balance of markings—sometimes there is not enough marking, and sometimes there is too much color. As a result, red and stag red are colors more frequently seen in show rings.

You might wonder what is meant by the disqualification of a thumb mark. This mark is a patch of black or chocolate hair that is completely surrounded by the rust-red coloring. It is located on the front of the lower front leg between the foot and the wrist. This patch of black or chocolate must appear to be an island within the "sea" of rust-red. Markings are not of consequence for the pet owner, of course, and many puppies with other excellent breed characteristics are available as pets due to incorrect or inadequate markings.

Thin coats are seen more often today, a problem breeders need to watch carefully. It is commonly believed that these thin coats are color-linked with the blue color gene, which is one reason that this color is not permitted in the AKC registry (although they are admitted for registration in the United Kingdom).

Many breeds grow coats on a continuing basis, but Min Pins do not. Coats will often appear thin due to periodic shedding.

GAIT—The forelegs and hind legs move parallel, with feet turning neither in nor out. The hackney-like action is a high-stepping, reaching, free and easy gait in which the front leg moves straight forward and in front of the body, and the foot bends at the

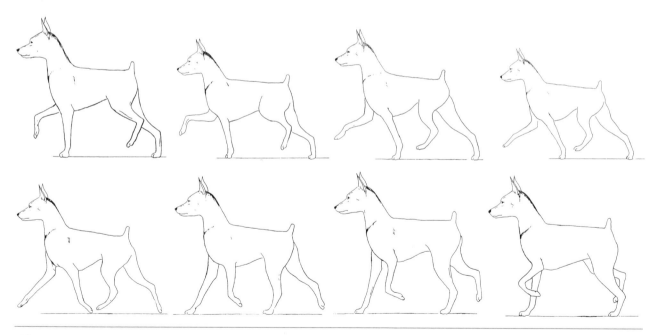

This series of eight drawings from the MPCA Illustrated Standard *shows the stage-by-stage progress of a correct hackney-like action.*

The Min Pin is forever watchful, even when guarding a watermelon.
(Photograph by Warfield)

wrist. The dog drives smoothly and strongly from the rear. The head and tail are carried high.

The reason the standard calls for a "hackney-like" action is that the true hackney pony action was not exactly what the Min Pin breeders wanted. The hackney pony has a straight stifle and long hocks, which give it little or no drive from the rear to supply good push behind the forward motion. The desirable action in the Min Pin was actually the stylish front action, especially the bend or break at the wrist. However, there had to be strong forward movement in the dog, so the standard was written with the requirement of a well-angulated stifle and short hocks.

THE COMPLETE PICTURE

Soundness of body, compact size, alert nature, self-assurance and devotion as a guardian and companion all present themselves in a handy Toy package. This is the essence of the Miniature Pinscher.

This 7-year-old black-and-rust dog has a coat that is just in the midst of shedding. (Photograph by Stamm)

(Photograph by Mary Bloom)

CHAPTER FOUR

Finding Your Miniature Pinscher— Puppy, Adult or Rescue

"The Min Pin's fondness for home and master is exceptional."
—AMERICAN KENNEL CLUB, *THE COMPLETE DOG BOOK,* 19th EDITION REVISED
(HOWELL BOOK HOUSE, 1997)

If you have decided that the Miniature Pinscher is just the right breed for you and your family, you need to answer a few questions before you go looking for your new family member. Here are some of the issues to consider:

- How do I find a responsible breeder?

- What is a rescue program?

- Will I qualify for ownership?

- Which dog should I take?

Fortunately, Min Pins are very good mothers, as evidenced by this red female taking care of her six puppies. (Photo by Denetre)

WHERE SHOULD YOU LOOK FOR YOUR NEW DOG?

Whether you have decided on a pet or a show prospect, you will need to obtain the names of reputable, responsible breeders in your area. You can obtain this information through the Miniature Pinscher Club of America or the American Kennel Club (see Appendix A, "Organizations and More Information"). The MPCA Breeder Referral Service is free. Breeders listed with the service are all members of MPCA and are bound by the Club's Code of Ethics (see Appendix B, "The Miniature Pinscher Club of America Code of Ethics"). Breeders are located throughout the United States as well as in several other countries.

When you have a list of breeders, start making appointments with several of them to meet and see their dogs and to view the environment in which the dogs are kept. Finding the right dog for you is a long process, not something you should expect to do on a whim some Saturday afternoon. You may be tempted by those ads in the newspaper, but your safest route is through a reputable breeder, and that will take time—lots of time. You will have questions. The breeder will have questions. And the search will not be easy. The hardest part is seeing irresistible puppies and learning to resist them!

WHAT IS A RESPONSIBLE BREEDER?

If you call a breeder and he says he'll meet you somewhere other than his home to show you dogs or puppies, go no further with him. Anyone who will not let you see the conditions under which his dogs live and evaluate the cleanliness and health of his dogs is not a responsible breeder. This would be equivalent to buying a puppy off the street corner. Beware!

Carefully Planned Breedings

A responsible breeder will never breed a litter without considering the betterment of the breed. Each litter is planned to improve the quality of the

Very young Min Pin puppies look a lot like puppies of other breeds. As they grow a bit older, their ears will come erect and they will begin to take on their Min Pin characteristics. (Photograph by Walton)

A Few Good Dogs

A reliable breeder will not have lots and lots of dogs; he will show you what he has for sale, and his dogs and their surroundings will be clean and neat. He will usually have at least the dam of the litter on the premises, and sometimes he will also have the sire. (Often people go to other parts of the country to breed their bitch and do not actually own the sire of the puppies; this is common practice among show people and responsible breeders.) The breeder should be knowledgeable about the breed and should have the betterment of the breed as his primary goal. He should be aware of health problems in the breed and should have lots of information on hand to share with a prospective buyer.

Genetic Testing

A responsible breeder will be willing to give the buyer certifications and test results for heritable disorders to indicate that both the sire and the dam are free from defects at that time. Disorders that

breeding stock, resulting in healthy puppies whose physical attributes are based on the ideals presented in the breed standard.

Commonly a litter will include some puppies that are not show-quality but that are ideal as companion pets. There *is* something for everyone.

GOOD NEIGHBOR POLICIES

Your neighbors might have a darling Min Pin. In fact, that might be what got you interested in the breed. But unless your neighbors are knowledgeable about health and soundness issues in the breed, it is probably safer to go to a recognized, reputable breeder rather than getting a dog from your friends next door. The Min Pin has a long life. Suppose something goes wrong with a puppy you get when Mitzie is bred to Fritz, who lives down the street? Unfortunately, many friendships have broken over disputes about dogs. A good policy is to enjoy your neighbor's dog, but get your puppy somewhere else.

develop later in life, such as Progressive Retinal Atrophy, must be assessed yearly and must be registered with the Canine Eye Research Foundation (CERF). These results and certifications are the breeder's best possible guarantee that your puppy or young adult is free of genetic defects. If a defect shows up on your dog later, it likely will be one that just slipped by the security guards. Should that be the case, a responsible breeder will work with you on returning or replacing your dog—even as far as refunding your money.

Mentoring

Most good breeders do not want their dogs to end up in shelters or a rescue situation. They want you to take dogs *out* of rescue, not put them into it. Along these lines, a reputable breeder will be willing to spend lots of time with you before and after your purchase to answer questions, provide information, advise on behavior problems and help with just about anything that might come up in the process of raising and owning a Min Pin.

In fact, this breeder will probably be happy to talk endlessly about the dogs. He will give you more specific details about the care and maintenance of your dog than you could find in any reading material. He will never abandon dogs or bitches just because they have gone beyond breeding age or productivity. A responsible breeder's home is usually full of aging pensioners.

A responsible breeder is someone you can trust because he comes through a proper referral source. He is someone who is honest with you about

A good breeder wants you to enjoy a lifetime of love with your dog and will help you along the way in raising your Min Pin. (Photograph by Mary Bloom)

what it's like to live with a Min Pin—he'll tell you all the joys and all the hazards. A responsible breeder will be there to support and advise you throughout the life of your dog.

Documentation

Every responsible breeder will provide you with a sales contract and detailed paperwork that describes your dog's lineage and registration status. The paperwork you have a right to expect is described in detail in a later section of this chapter.

WILL YOU QUALIFY FOR OWNERSHIP?

When you start on your journey to Min Pin ownership, don't be offended if the breeders you contact ask you lots of questions. You will be on the receiving end of an interview, but don't feel annoyed because your ownership credentials are being questioned or explored. If you stop and think about it, this process should be reassuring because it means that you have contacted a responsible, reputable breeder who *cares* about where his puppies go—and to whom. As a potential owner, *you* are very important to the responsible breeder.

Get Ready for a Grilling

After answering all your questions, the breeder will want to interview you, the buyer. Many people seem to believe that they are doing the breeder a favor by buying one of his puppies, but that's not necessarily the case.

The first question will probably be something like, "Why do you want a Min Pin?" That will be followed by, "Have you had a Min Pin before?" and "Where did you get my name?" And it goes on from there.

GETTING A DOG SHOULD BE A FAMILY PROJECT

Before you start the process of looking for a puppy, be sure that all family members are in agreement that getting a dog will provide enjoyment and pleasure. If anyone has reservations about the purchase of a pet, don't go forward. Remember that even if the dog will be "your" pet, everyone else in the home has to live with Sparky, too. And Sparky will have to live with them—that's not a happy situation if Sparky isn't genuinely wanted. *Never* consider getting a dog to help a child get over a fear of them. That will spell disaster, and no reputable breeder will sell a dog to you if he discovers that this is your motivation.

This little girl is quite calm and happy holding three wiggly red Min Pin pups. She's not afraid of them, and they certainly don't appear to be uncomfortable with her. (Photograph by Stamm)

A breeder needs to get an idea of what kind of home you will provide for a Min Pin and whether he thinks the Min Pin is the right breed for your household. He'll want to know if someone will be home with the dog all day. He will want to know if you have a really secure yard—not just fenced, but *secure*. Remember, Min Pins can be escape artists—over or under, they don't care as long as they get to the other side!

If you have small children, the breeder will probably want to meet them to evaluate how they will handle the dog. Min Pins are tough, but they can also break.

Many breeders will sell you a pet *only* if you agree to spay or neuter the dog. This request applies for a pet-quality dog only. (To be shown, a dog must be intact. Thus, if you're buying a dog to show, this will not be an issue.)

Chief among the breeder's questions will be inquiries about what you expect from a Min Pin. Where did you see or hear about a Min Pin? What is your lifestyle? Are you a quiet household, or will you appreciate the activity that you will have with a Min Pin?

As you can see, you will get a series of questions that start out with why, why, why. Remember, breeders care about what happens to their dogs.

One breeder states, "I like to be asked a zillion questions by the new prospective buyer. If people call and just want to know if I've got any puppies and how much are they, I tend to get turned off. I like it when the buyer has already done his homework and has read up on the breed, or at least knows someone who owns one and knows a little

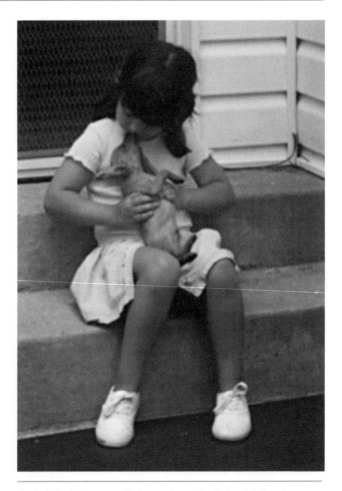

This Min Pin puppy is focused on his little girl, but he might just as quickly jump out of her lap. Even though the child is not restraining him, she has had proper supervision and is sitting on a low step to hold the dog. That way, if he leaps away from her, he will not be likely to injure himself. (Photograph by Stamm)

about Min Pins before calling. I have to see the prospective buyers interact with the puppies and my older dogs to see how they deal with a Min Pin."

A knowledgeable breeder will carefully observe how the dogs respond to the buyer. The dogs will tell the breeder whether the buyer is one with whom they can bond. The adult dogs also will indicate whether the buyer is trustworthy. Remember that Min Pins are great guardians. There are stories of adult dogs putting themselves firmly between the breeder and the prospective buyer, indicating mistrust. These are important indicators, and breeders almost always pay attention to them and accept them as valid.

Another breeder has specific, firm criteria for acceptable buyers: "Single adults, families with children well over the age of 5, with a fenced backyard a must. The dog must be a house dog first, with backyard privileges, having shade, shelter and plenty of fresh water."

Min Pins are energetic, and breeders will look for owners who are committed to caring for an active dog. (Photograph by Mary Bloom)

Covering other angles, another breeder demands: "Someone who is willing to take on the responsibility of a very energetic dog and be willing to actively work with that dog to fit the buyer's lifestyle. Min Pins need attention, and if you are not willing to devote some time to your dog, then maybe a dog is not the right pet for you. It is a commitment for as long as that dog lives, and that is a long time with a Min Pin. The dog deserves the best in quality of life."

Breeders do not want to let a dog go to a family that comes through the door squabbling; whiny kids or loud parents will make a poor impression. If there is any sign that family harmony is lacking, this will not be a good home for a Min Pin. If parents allow the kids to tease or bully a sibling, for example, they will also allow them to tease a dog. After all, if people can't be kind to each other, why would anyone think they would be kind to a dog?

Breeders are also not inclined to let a Min Pin go to a household with large dogs or dogs that are known to be dog-aggressive. Regardless of the large dog's history of compatibility, when the big dog gets old and cranky, it might snap at a small dog—and that would be the end of the Min Pin. Obviously, a resident dog that has shown signs of aggression toward other dogs is a poor companion for a Miniature Pinscher as well.

LET EACH DOG HAVE HIS DAY

It may be tempting for a variety of reasons, but it is not a good idea to get a Min Pin puppy to replace an elderly dog before it dies. If the old dog is too old and inactive to play with a puppy, then he's too old to be harassed by a puppy. Let the older dog live out his life in peace, and then get a puppy.

WHICH DOG SHOULD YOU TAKE?

Overall, look for healthy, outgoing puppies that are in good condition. Are they clean, bright-eyed and full of energy? Are the breeder's facilities clean, secure and well-maintained? Can you see the mother of the puppies? If she is not available, ask why not. Ask about health issues that concern the breed. If any of these questions, or questions about testing and certification, have not been answered to your satisfaction, look for another breeder.

Choosing a Puppy

If you are allowed to choose from a litter, do the puppies come up to you without any signs of shyness? Even if they all do, there will probably be one that will just immediately own you; your hearts will connect, and you will be pals for life. If you find that your choice isn't absolutely instant, take some time to watch the puppies interact. You want the puppy that is playful and inquisitive, but not aggressive or overly assertive with his littermates.

A word of caution: Make every effort to resist the sad little fellow that hides or hangs back from

you and his littermates. This is not typical of a Min Pin, but it could happen. All the love in the world might not be enough to turn that little fellow around. You are entitled to start out with an outgoing, self-assured, happy puppy.

When You Don't Have a Choice

Very often buyers get a puppy that the breeder has selected for them. Breeders make every effort to match puppies with owners so that the relationship will be compatible. In fact, puppies are shipped all over the world to new owners who rely with confidence on the breeder of their choice. This emphasizes the need to be extra-cautious when selecting a breeder. If you receive your puppy sight unseen, a reputable breeder will follow up with you to be certain that you and the puppy are settling in together. If changes have to be made, the breeder will work with you toward an appropriate outcome.

You may not see an entire litter, as breeders often keep puppies long enough to select any show prospects. You will then see older puppies that did not turn out to be show dogs. That does not mean that they won't make wonderful pets, though, so don't be discouraged.

If you are buying a show dog, you will very likely depend on your chosen breeder to make the selection for you and to guide you through subsequent showing and breeding of your Min Pin.

BUYING A PET PUPPY

If you're looking for a dog as a companion, ask the breeder about spaying or neutering the dog. As mentioned earlier, it's likely that you will have to promise to have the dog altered at the appropriate time. The breeder should be able to provide you with some guidance in this issue. Be sure to inquire about what shots the puppy has had and to get a written confirmation of this information to bring to your veterinarian. Also find out what kind of food the puppy has been eating. If the breeder doesn't give you some food to take with you, be sure to purchase the same brand and to start the dog off on that particular food. If you want to switch brands later, do so gradually. A new home is very exciting (and a bit traumatic), and you don't want your new friend to start off with an upset stomach.

There's no need to crop the ears of a companion dog, and breeders will be happy to avoid this expense. Because ears are usually cropped at about 16 weeks of age, your pet Miniature Pinscher won't have to wait around at the breeder's for this event. This means that you can bring your puppy home during his critical formative weeks, around 7 to 12 weeks of age. During this time, puppies develop strong bonds—if your puppy is with you, you'll be the one with whom he bonds. Sometimes breeders will not decide on show-quality

These four pups in an igloo seem to be saying, "Are you my new person? Are you going to take me home? Do I have to leave my buddies? Why don't you take all of us?" (Photograph by Warfield)

versus pet-quality puppies before the dogs are about 16 weeks old. If this is the case, ask the breeder about why he has decided that this puppy, whose ears will not be cropped, is not of show quality. Does that mean that the puppy is not a good Min Pin? That's not necessarily the case, but it is good to ask so that you have the full picture.

FINDING A SHOW PROSPECT

Until a dog has been out in the show ring, struts his stuff and does some winning, he is *not* a show dog—he is only a show *prospect*. That is all the breeder can guarantee, and that is all for which you can hold the breeder responsible.

If you want a pet, there is no need to make the puppy go through the stress and discomfort of having his ears cropped. (Photo by Westover)

Breeders often have a good idea about whether a puppy will succeed in the show ring. Some dogs have a natural talent, such as this red puppy standing on a couch and looking for all the world as if he is ready to go into the show ring.

A breeder will have measured his dogs against the commonly accepted growth chart (see Chapter 12, "To Breed or Not to Breed") so that he can make an educated guess as to whether the puppy will fall within the accepted height limitations. Most indicative, he will have a *reputation.*

If you want a show dog and are serious about getting into the Min Pin fancy, you will have done a great deal more homework than the people looking for an adorable, lively pet. You will have to go to many dog shows and talk to many breeders. You will have to study the breed standard, watch the Min Pin classes being judged and decide on the type of Min Pin you prefer. Type is only one element of breed character; it is the physical appearance of the dog, its make and shape, and its size and proportion. Does the dog look at you when standing still and say, "I am a Miniature

Pinscher"? If so, that is the type you want. The next step is to look for breeders who are producing that type of dog.

Don't forget that there is more to a Min Pin than how he looks standing. He also must have the remaining elements of breed character: personality, temperament, attitude, soundness of movement and mentality. He must have that active, sort of aggressive, terrier-like personality that suited his original function.

Given all these considerations, the search is on for the one special Min Pin that is right for you and that you can afford. Actually, if you are truly serious about your intentions, the breeders of your choice will probably be more than willing to work with you on price. They'll also be happy to provide you with a lot of support to help you get into the show ring and enjoy a show career with your selected Min Pin.

SHOW PROSPECT OR PET: WHAT TO LOOK FOR

Look for an active, non-shivery puppy. The dog should be healthy, with non-weepy eyes and nose; should have a shiny coat; should have had at least one puppy shot and a worm check; should be free of fleas; should show no signs of skin problems; and should be at least 8 weeks old. The puppy should come right up to sniff your fingers. He should have bright eyes and a solid little body. If the puppy is more than 8 weeks old, he should have had any additional shots and wormings that meet your veterinarian's schedule of health maintenance.

In a Min Pin, essentially what you see is what you get. There's no long hair to cover up faults or structure, and there are some visible signs of quality. (Photograph by Westover)

Most breeders will offer a guarantee of health or return or exchange for ten days after purchase. New owners are encouraged to immediately take the dog to a veterinarian for an independent evaluation. If the buyer does not have a veterinarian, most breeders are able to provide the names of two or three acceptable practices in the buyer's immediate area.

Does Color Make a Difference?

Color should not make a difference if you are in search of a pet Min Pin. However, some coat problems supposedly are linked to the blue color. Be sure to discuss this thoroughly with the breeders you contact if you happen to want a blue. A responsible breeder will be able and willing to tell you the background health history of the pup you are considering. If a breeder will not discuss health problems with blues, find another breeder.

Are there other differences among the colors? Some breeders say chocolates are easier to train; some say that black-and-rust dogs are more laid-back; some say that reds are more hyperactive. There is no consensus of opinion, so we can only surmise that these kinds of comments are based on isolated personal experiences. And—a major point—these differences may be related to inherited factors only and have nothing to do with color.

It all boils down to the fact that you should go with the color and type you happen to find most exciting. Your dog should be exactly what you want to see when you awaken every day.

What About Papers?

Most people who buy a purebred dog receive papers along with the purchase. What these papers are and what they mean can vary. Most often this includes a pedigree, a family tree of the breeding behind the dog or puppy you have just bought or acquired. Looking at the pedigree of your dog *before* you acquire the dog can tell you whether the pedigree represents proper breeding practices and also can tell you something about the quality and intelligence of your dog's ancestors.

A pedigree is *not* a registration paper. It is an important document, but it is only a document that tells you the sire and dam of your dog, as well as three to five generations of its ancestors. A pedigree is *not* proof of ownership.

A Dog's Pedigree

If you have bought your dog from a reputable, responsible breeder, the dog's pedigree is one major part of the series of papers you will want for your dog. The pedigree should give you a lot of information about your dog and his ancestors. This should be the breeder's representation of a family tree that you can be proud of, but if you can't decipher the components of the pedigree, it will have little or no meaning for you. You need a translation of the pedigree jargon to unlock the mysteries of breeding practices.

The names on the pedigree are the names of the sire and dam (dad and mom) of your dog. These names are the two at the far left of the pedigree. The top half of the page will tell you all the names of your dog's sire's family. Just to the

top-right of the sire's name will be the name of *his* sire, which is your dog's grandfather. Just below the sire's name will be the name of his dam, which is your dog's paternal grandmother. This branching is repeated for as many generations as your pedigree covers, telling you the names of all of the sire's ancestors and each set of parents.

The bottom half of the page will tell you all the same type of information for your dog's dam's family. As the pedigree moves toward the right side of the page (which means backward in time and breeding), columns of dogs' names will appear and this can be very confusing for a beginner. There's an age-old saying about a picture being worth a thousand words, and words could never be truer than when talking about a pedigree. Look at the pedigree of "Sizzle" for an illustration.

- **Registered names** Registered names are the names that usually appear on a pedigree. Very often breeders will adopt a name for their kennel. If they have done this, all the dogs they breed will carry that kennel name. In the sample pedigree, Sizzle carries the kennel name Whitehouse. Unless you have read and studied a lot before you acquire your puppy, it is not likely that you will recognize kennel names. As a clue, look for repeats of the prefix name throughout the pedigree.

- **Call names** Although it is not intended to confuse you further, many breeders use a call name (or nickname) for their dogs in addition to their registered kennel names. A conversation that mixes call names with kennel names can sound like something from an alien planet.

The pedigree of Ch. Whitehouse's Hot Damm Here I Am ("Sizzle"), the 1998 winner of the MPCA National Specialty, tells you a lot about his background.

In addition to looking at a dog's lineage when you search for a puppy, ask yourself whether this is the right little guy for your home. (Photograph by Mary Bloom)

With any luck, your pedigree will include the dogs' call names in parentheses after their kennel names.

Very often you will see the same name appearing at various places in a pedigree. It could be that that is the name of a great dog or bitch, and its contribution to the breed might become apparent in your dog's pedigree. There are two possibilities here: Repeated appearance of a dog's name can be a good thing, or it could spell trouble. Here's why.

- **Line breeding** A breeding practice called line breeding usually means breeding that stays pretty much within an established line of dogs. One example is a good dog who has been bred to his granddaughter or his niece or his grandmother. In human terms, this would be unacceptable, and humans looking at a pedigree often think that this is inbreeding— it's not. In the same way, a bitch might be bred to her grandfather or her nephew or her grandson. Do not be confused by this approach to breeding. In fact, it is through line breeding that many great dogs are created. Line breeding has been the accepted established practice of livestock breeders for as long as there have been registries established for beef, sheep or swine.

Line breeding is another way breeders use to set a type, or a representation of what they think is the best-looking dog of that breed with the best temperament and physical characteristics. When a breeder's dogs can be recognized on sight as being of a particular type, that breeder has established a line—hence, "line breeding."

Look again at Sizzle's pedigree. This dog is the result of good line breeding. The approach pulls together a concentration of excellent dogs that are recognized as producers of top-quality Miniature Pinschers.

Staying with Sizzle's pedigree, notice that his sire, Ch. Whitehouse's Oh Danny Boy, was the result of what is called an out-cross, which is another perfectly acceptable approach to breeding. Ch. Elan's Shiloh von Whitehouse was introduced into the line via Danny Boy and also via Ch. Whitehouse's Bundle of Joy. The results were excellent for breeder Judy White.

- **In-breeding**   However, be sure to avoid a dog that is the product of in-breeding. In-breeding is the very close breeding of dogs. For example, it might be mother to son; father to daughter; brother to sister (littermates); or half-brother to half-sister (those having the same sire or the same dam). For example, if Sizzle were to be bred to his mother, that would be in-breeding.

- **Out-crossing**   Another type of pedigree in which there is no line breeding is called scatter-shot. There is no line breeding here; there is only careful out-crossing of one good dog to another, based on each dog's heritage. Because the pedigree is based on out-crosses, there is less chance of encountering some of the genetic anomalies that might be troubling a breed.

  With out-cross breeding, the breeder gets the good qualities of the other dog but also gets the hidden faults, problems that may not be apparent on the surface. Out-crossing is always a gamble, but when things go right, the result is good quality with good health.

- **Certifications**   A dog's pedigree may show documentation of health certifications. Be sure to

ask the breeders you contact about any genetic problems in Min Pins and what tests, if any, are required to certify that their dogs are free of these problems. You might run into certifications from any or all of the following:

- **Hip and elbow problems**   The Orthopedic Foundation of America (OFA) issues a number or a grade, such as Excellent, Good or Fair. This test is done by X ray once in a lifetime but must be done after a dog is 2 years of age. In some breeds, the test also examines the patellas, or kneecaps.

- **Eye problems**   The Canine Eye Research Foundation issues this certification with a number and a date. This test is done by a certified ophthalmologist and must be done *annually*. The test checks for potential problems such as progressive retinal atrophy, cataracts and other eye abnormalities that do or might lead to blindness.

- **Von Willebrand's Disease**   This DNA test is done with a home testing kit and a lab results report once in a lifetime. The test can be done at any age.

- **Thyroid function**   Function should be within normal limits on all scales. This is tested by a veterinarian with a simple blood test and a lab report.

- **Championships and other titles**   Many people are impressed by the number of champions that appear in a pedigree. Champions indicate a certain level of quality behind the dog you are thinking of acquiring. Also, dogs do not become

Champions if they do not have good temperament and soundness. A wide variety of possible titles might appear in your dog's pedigree; for a listing of titles available to Min Pins, see Appendix C, "Titles Available to the Miniature Pinscher."

If other abbreviations appear on the pedigree, ask the breeder for their meaning, or contact the American Kennel Club, Inc., Customer Service, 5580 Centerview Dr., Suite 200, Raleigh, NC 27606-3390.

AKC Registration Application

To register your dog, the sire and dam of the puppy must have been registered. Some breeders register all puppies in a litter in order to put their kennel names on the dog's registered name. For each puppy in a registered litter, the American Kennel Club provides a separate application for registration of that puppy. If the breeder does not register all puppies in a litter, this will be the form on which the breeder will transfer ownership to you. You must complete the form within six months and send it to the AKC with the proper fee. A few weeks later, you will receive the regular registration certificate indicating that you are the owner of your Min Pin.

AKC Registration Certificate

Two forms of registration certificates exist. (Note that if you're buying or taking on an adult dog, you should receive his registration certificate when you get him.)

- **Regular registration** The regular AKC registration certificate is white with a purple border around it. This certifies your dog's name, your name and address as owner, the name and address of the breeder, the sire and dam of your dog and their AKC registration numbers, your dog's date of birth, his sex and color and his individual registration number. Keep this in a safe place—it is similar to the registration for your car!

- **Limited registration** The limited registration is a white certificate with a light orange border around it. When a breeder, for reasons of breed health or quality, believes that a dog or bitch should not be bred, the limited registration is one way of assuring that puppies from that animal will not be registered with the American Kennel Club.

A Bill of Sale

If you do not receive a registration application or a registration certificate that's properly completed by the breeder, you should at least receive a bill of sale for the dog. This should list the sire and dam of your dog, their AKC registration numbers, the date the puppy was born, the puppy's sex and color, the name and address of the breeder, your name and address and the date you bought the dog.

If the breeder or seller is not willing to provide you with one of the forms of transfer mentioned here, *do not* buy the dog! Sometimes a breeder who is naming each individual dog in the litter does not yet have the registration certificates back from AKC. If that is the case, the breeder should provide you with a signed interim bill of sale. You must have one form or another that attests to your ownership of the dog.

Puppy Sales Contracts

You will be expected to conform to the conditions the breeder sets forth in a sales contract. This contract might state that the dog must be spayed or neutered, or it might contain showing or even breeding rights. If you are presented with such a contract, read it carefully. When signed by both parties, this contract can become legally binding. Be absolutely sure of what the sales conditions are. Min Pin breeders are more likely to insist that you spay or neuter your dog than to insist that you actually *breed* your dog. If the breeder knows you and trusts you, there might be a breeding arrangement, but again be absolutely clear about the terms of the agreement.

Do not allow yourself to be rushed into signing the sales contract before you understand its provisions and implications. In many states, you have the option of returning merchandise (in this case, your adorable Min Pin) within a few days if you change your mind about the sale provisions or contract. Consult your State Department of Consumer Affairs if you have questions.

FINDING A PET ADULT MIN PIN

Quite often breeders are looking for good homes for their retired dogs or bitches. This means that the dogs have finished their show careers or that the bitches have had one or two litters and are not

to be bred again. Or, perhaps the dogs have had to be spayed or neutered because of some unexpected illness or injury. These adults are great for an elderly adult person. In fact, a charming dog may just not like to be shown. When this occurs, a breeder might look for someone to care for the dog.

There are two sides to the coin of buying or adopting an adult dog. On the one hand, Min Pins are loving dogs and will adore anyone who is kind to them. And with their puppy-like playfulness, they never seem to really grow up.

On the other hand, Min Pins also become very bonded to their owners. Helping an adult dog make the transition from his prior owner to you can require a lot of skill and, above all, *patience*. You might find that the dog goes through an

The older Min Pin can love just as much as a puppy. People who adopt retired show dogs wouldn't give up their dogs for anything. (Photograph by Westover)

adjustment period that includes depression, misbe-
havior and downright rejection of you. If you have
enough love in your heart and are the right person
for the adult dog, things will work out within a
few weeks.

But what if things do *not* work out? You and
that dog just might not be meant for each other.
That doesn't mean that the dog is bad or that you
shouldn't have a Min Pin; sometimes it just works
that way. Go back to the breeder who sold you the
dog. Most likely, the breeder has been in close
touch with you to see if the adjustment is going
well—if there's a problem, the breeder will almost
always try to work out a solution.

You must remember that this dog will live to
be 16 years old or more. If you and the dog don't
bond, and if you don't return him to the breeder,
he will end up in rescue or, worse, in a shelter. The
better choice is to have a few sad days and take
him back to the breeder. Maybe you want to get a
puppy, or perhaps just look for a different adult
dog. Work with the breeder—when you end up
with a Min Pin who bonds with you, you will be
one happy owner. It's worth the time and effort.

RESCUE PROGRAMS

The Miniature Pinscher Club of America operates
a nationwide rescue program. Members and other
Min Pin lovers around the country open their
homes to Min Pins that are found in shelters or
that are without homes for a number of reasons,
including the death of an owner, an owner's need
to move into convalescent care or (infrequently) an
owner's loss of interest in the breed or inability to
form a lasting relationship with a dog.

For detailed information on the MPCA rescue
program, and for the rescue contact nearest you,
see Appendix A, "Organizations and More
Information."

Rescued Dogs

Sometimes Min Pins turn up in shelters. Usually
this is because the dog was not bought from a
reputable breeder who followed up on the purchase, or because the buyers did not do their
homework on the breed before their purchase.
Perhaps the dog was expected to stay at home all

DON'T OVERLOOK SHELTERS

If you find a Min Pin to adopt at a shelter, you will probably pay an adoption fee and will be
required to have the dog spayed or neutered at an appropriate age. Depending on your location,
these costs can range up to $100 or more. If you do get your Min Pin from a shelter, be sure to con-
tact the MPCA for the names of breeders in your area so that you'll have someone who can answer
your questions and mentor you through the process of owning a Min Pin. (See Appendix A,
"Organizations and More Information," for contact numbers.)

If you remember your reading, you know by now that the Min Pin needs company—if you can't be available very regularly, another Min Pin, another dog or, in desperate times, even a cat will do. (Photograph by Westover)

day alone while its owners went off to work. This situation never works well for a Min Pin.

The Rescuers

All over the country, responsible and caring breeders and Min Pin owners get involved in rescuing—that is, giving foster care to—Min Pins that have been abandoned for any reason. As you might guess, some rescued dogs have shown behavior problems. The dedicated people who give their time, money and patience to rehabilitating and rescuing dogs and finding proper homes for them are true Min Pin lovers. These people work very hard to see that the dog placed through the rescue program makes a good adjustment and that the dog is right for the people who adopt him. Again, mentoring is involved before, during and after the adoption.

The Story of Cody

The tenacity of dedicated Min Pin rescuers and their follow-up on dogs placed in new homes is illustrated by the story of Cody. This story comes from a dedicated breeder in Southern California:

We had a neutered red male called Cody come from a local county. The family was in tears about leaving the dog. They said he was the perfect dog for the first year, and then for some reason he started biting. The only one in the family the dog hadn't bitten was their son.

When they told me the story, I let them know that if we couldn't bring the dog around, we might

have to put him down—we couldn't risk putting a dog out for adoption who might take a kid's face off. They understood.

We worked with Cody for over a month, and we were met with hostility every time we tried to handle him. Finally, we decided to give him one more week, but we decided euthanasia was the only thing we could do.

The next morning, a big truck pulled up in front of the house, and the driver wanted to buy a puppy. I didn't have any puppies, so he asked if I had an adult dog he could buy. I told him all I had was a rescue dog that was a biter. He wanted to see the dog. I told him I couldn't get the dog out of the kennel, so he said he'd go to the kennel to see him.

As soon as Cody spotted the guy, he started barking and crying, and jumping up and down wagging his tail. The guy went into the kennel, and the dog was all over him, jumping on him and kissing him. Needless to say, Cody had found a home.

Shortly afterward, Cody's former owner called. I told the woman about the truck driver and said that he was about 5 feet tall with long blond hair and very slight in build. She said, "My gosh! You just described my son, the only person Cody liked."

Cody and his friend stop by to see us now and again. The dog still loves the trucking life and still hates my husband and me, but oh well—it was a good adoption.

That rescue story had a happy ending. It once again emphasizes the fact that Min Pins will become very strongly attached to one person and maybe not to anyone else, even family members.

Part of that problem is the nature of the breed. However, there's a good chance that Cody was not well incorporated into the family that owned him. It's likely that he was considered the sole property of the son and was not expected to show respect or affection to other family members. Unfortunately, this could have been prevented if the original family had been guided with sufficient mentoring or had gone to some puppy training classes while Cody was learning how to be a dog in the world.

As mentioned before, rescue volunteers work very hard to prepare dogs for a new home and also work hard to select a new owner that will be just right for the rescued Min Pin. (And not all rescue dogs are problem pets—some people just don't realize what it means to share their home with a dog.) An adult Min Pin can make a wonderful companion. Don't overlook the chance to adopt a rescue dog in your search for the dog of your dreams.

(Photograph by Mary Bloom)

Living with a Miniature Pinscher

"Those first days with 'Mr. Min Pin' are critical for you and the dog."
—MARGARET BAGSHAW

Let's assume that you have done all your correct preparation for the great event of bringing home the Min Pin. You have read all about the breed, you've attended dog shows and talked with exhibitors and breeders, and you and your family have given the acquisition of the Min Pin a great deal of thought.

This is *not* the time to sit back and just wait for the happy day. You have work to do! You will need to decorate with Min Pin preparations. Be sure you get all the things mentioned in the following sections; this list is approved by the Miniature Pinscher Club of America. Much experienced thought has gone into preparing this list; leaving out any one component would be like leaving the sugar out of your favorite cookie recipe. Trust the experts!

Everyone has agreed that the Miniature Pinscher is for you! Based on that, you have contacted reputable breeders, and after many visits, you and a breeder have agreed on the puppy or adult dog that you will be bringing home. (Photograph by Matheson)

IMPORTANT SUPPLIES FOR YOUR NEW ARRIVAL

What do I get? And how much? And where? This next section answers all your questions on the recommended supplies, so get out your shopping list and a pen.

Dog Food

The breeder will probably send home a small supply of dog food along with your dog. However, you should have your own supply on hand, so ask the breeder exactly what to get, and then—you

guessed it—get that and *only* that. Do not change one iota of the dog's food from what he has been accustomed to eating. That includes any treats. As mentioned in the last chapter, changing homes is a big deal to your dog. He'll be excited by the new environment, the new people and the new smells. The last thing he needs is to have to adjust to a new diet.

Although we'll discuss nutrition in more detail in Chapter 7, "The Care and Feeding of Your Miniature Pinscher," take note now that you may find your Min Pin acting finicky. If he seems to develop a disdain for his food, your first response is to make sure that he's feeling all right. Assuming that he's not sick, he could well be trying to get you to offer something different—perhaps some of the steak you took off the grill. If you *once* give in to his "I don't like this food" pretense, you will be driving yourself crazy trying to find something he *will* like. Rule of thumb: Don't do it!

Feed your dog the right food in the right amount. After ten minutes pick up the dish; if there are leftovers, throw them away. The dog will eat when he gets hungry. This should take only a day or two. You control your dog's diet—he does not. By doing so, you're not only assuring that your dog is eating healthful food, but you're also helping to enforce that you are Alpha—the number one person—in the dog's life. This is very important for all your interactions with your dog.

Dishes

We're not talking about Spode china here. Just ask the breeder what kind of dishes the dog has had for his food and water, and then go to the store and buy exactly the same kind. They might be stainless steel, which is good because it goes happily through the dishwasher and is more sanitary than other surfaces. Plastic dishes are not recommended as they sometimes serve as an invitation to chew. If you do buy plastic dishes, be sure they are not brittle and that small pieces cannot break off. If swallowed, these pieces could injure your dog seriously.

Crate or Kennel

No matter how big or how small, no matter what his intended lifestyle, no matter what *your* lifestyle, every dog must have a crate. A dog's crate is not a cage; it is not cruel. The crate becomes the dog's den, his safe place. The crate also is a secure place for him to ride in the car or to be left at home for short periods of time. In addition, a crate will solve many of your potential training problems. You and your dog will live happier lives if you get him a crate before he comes home. Most Min Pins are trained to a size 100 crate or a wire crate from puppyhood.

Different kinds of crates exist, and any kind will do as long as it is of a size that allows the dog to stand up with his head erect (don't forget to accommodate his adult size). Solid metal crates, however, are not recommended for Min Pins because they are too dark and gloomy. Instead, choose a fiberglass or hard plastic crate with wire inserts in the sides and wire doors. These are also approved by most airlines for air travel. Bench crates are the kind of crates that are required at shows where the dogs must be on display all day

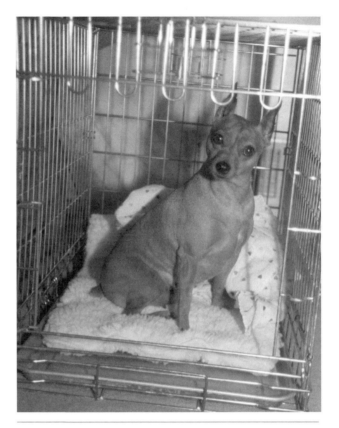

A wire crate lets your Min Pin feel a part of the action. (Photograph by Mary Bloom)

for the public to see. They have wire on all sides and the top, with a pan insert on the bottom. These crates are great for a Min Pin because they allow him to see everything that is going on around him. They might not protect him from drafts, though, so take your breeder's advice about the best kind of crate to get for your dog.

Be sure to have the crate on hand when you go to get your puppy or dog. If he is accustomed

A Tip on Traveling and Crates

If you take your Min Pin on an airplane, it's best that he ride in the cabin with you rather than in the cargo hold. He should have a carrying bag or case that will fit under the seat in front of you. Most allow one pet (sometimes more) inside the cabin on each flight; usually you must make a reservation ahead of time and pay an extra fee that varies but ranges upward from $50 per pet.

Min Pins like to burrow into and under any kind of bedding—yours or theirs—but the favorite is the snuggle sack. (Photograph by Matheson)

to a crate, he will feel safer on the trip home if he is in his crate. (Not only will he *feel* safer, but he'll *be* safer, too!)

Bedding

These days, we are fortunate to have machine-washable (and dryer-safe) sheepskin or sheepskin-like pads and blankets that make great bedding. Even if the dog has an accident in the crate or bed, the sheepskin material will absorb the fluid without soiling your dog. No matter how neatly you make your Min Pin's bed, though, he will rumple it up into a pile to suit himself. Just get used to it—that's the way *he* makes his bed. Be sure to have two or three sets of bedding so that you can change it regularly.

Exercise Pen with Lid

You will probably balk at this one, but it is essential and will serve many purposes. The pen, commonly called an X-pen, should be about 4 feet by 4 feet and 24 inches high. X-pens are made of the same wire sections used for bench crates and are easily collapsible. This pen can be put in your yard to allow the dog to remain unsupervised in a shaded area for a short time, if the temperature and humidity permit.

The 4 × 4 pen can also be made into a 2-foot-by-4-foot pen to put next to your bed (with the top on it) while you are housetraining the dog. The pen also can come into the room where the family congregates so that the dog can be with you but not roaming freely around the house, possibly looking for trouble.

Remember that if you want your Min Pin to stay in the pen, you will have to attach the lid to it firmly. Don't forget that the Min Pin is the Houdini of the dog world!

A Doggie Bed

Some people use the dog's crate, with the door removed, as his bed. Or, you can remove the top of a plastic crate and use the bottom half inside the X-pen as a bed. You have to decide which arrangement suits your lifestyle best. Most Min Pins, though, much prefer the kind of beds usually used for cats: a round bed with fleece inside.

Miniature Pinschers are creatures of comfort, and they seem to adore fleece pet beds. (Photograph by Mary Bloom)

weights; the type sold for cats should be sufficient for a Min Pin.

Toys

Min Pins like a lot of toys, but remember their terrier ancestors and do not give them plastic or rubber squeaky toys. The dog will "kill" the squeaker as soon as possible and might swallow it and get into trouble. Instead, look for toys made of plush, fleece-type fabric with the squeaker sewn inside the toy—at the least, it will take a dog longer to get to the squeaker. Other kinds of chew-toys are acceptable as well, so be sure to get a variety.

Collar and Leash

Take the breeder's advice about what kind of collar to use for your dog—cloth, leather or a fine choke chain. A relatively narrow collar is suitable for a Min Pin because he has a pretty little neck.

A lightweight, 6-foot leash is fine. Also available is what is commonly called a "bungee" leash, a retractable leash that allows your dog more freedom and a little of the independence Min Pins crave. These leashes require some practice to acquire the skill of stopping and retracting the leash when you want. This leash comes in various

SELECTING A VETERINARIAN

If you've never had a pet and don't have a relationship established with a local veterinarian, go shopping—yes, shopping. Retaining a veterinarian is about the same as finding a pediatrician for your baby: You are the consumer, and you have choices about your veterinarian.

Make a few calls, and set up appointments to meet with local veterinarians who have had Min Pin patients. After you have decided on one you like, let the doctor know that you will be getting a Min Pin and ask about procedures in case of an

Get your Min Pin some toys to keep him busy. If he has his own toys, he's less likely to use your slipper as a "chewy." (Photograph by Mary Bloom)

emergency. Make an appointment to have your dog examined shortly after you bring him home. You want your veterinarian to get to know your dog and to schedule remaining puppy shots and the like.

MAKE YOURSELF A SCHEDULE

The family should set up a schedule for when the dog will be fed, exercised and played with. The dog will need a reliable daily routine, and it will make life easier for you if you follow this schedule. There will be exceptions, of course, but try to make them rare. Min Pins require structure in their lives, and it is up to you to set the structure and then maintain it.

Make a clear decision about who in the family will take care of which doggy chores, and add those names to the schedule. When the schedule is set, write it down and post it where all family members can see it. The front of the refrigerator is a good place—almost everyone in the family visits that once a day.

PUPPY-PROOFING

Min Pins are inquisitive, and having a new home to explore will keep your puppy very busy. If you're a new dog owner, you'll be amazed at how creative dogs can be when it comes to finding the scrap of food under the table or the stray rubber band behind the desk. Keep your dog safe by thoroughly puppy-proofing the house before he comes through the door.

Preparing the Home

Pretend that you're having a toddler come to live with you, because that is very close to the truth. You will have to examine (and rearrange) your home so that the Min Pin will not be in danger— and so that your treasures won't, either!

Get down on your knees to check out life from your Min Pin's perspective. If it's on the floor, it's fair game! Be certain to put away all small objects that are out on tables, floors and counters.

Also be sure that electrical cords are not within reach; dogs love to chew on cords, and this is a very dangerous activity.

In spite of their small stature, Min Pins can reach high as well and are drawn like magnets to things that are no-nos. Be careful never to leave any medication out, and quickly retrieve any pill you drop on the floor, or your Min Pin will find it. As your dog gets older, he'll be slightly less likely to eat small objects.

Everything goes into a Min Pin puppy's mouth— panty hose, pencils, pens, crayons, dice from board games, paper clips, coins, lipstick and more.

Miniature Pinschers are very, very quick and can scoot out a door that is left ajar for only a second. It is recommended that you install framed screen doors on all doors that open to any unsecured area. The screen door can act like a safety net while you are coming and going. Check with a breeder or the MPCA for advice on correct types of doors.

Preparing the Yard

You will have to comb every inch of your yard and also check your fence and your gates. This is even more important than puppy-proofing your house because you certainly don't want your Min Pin to get out and run off down the street to face a potentially dire outcome. Pick up all small objects, replace any loose boards or wires and make

sure that your gate locks work very, very well. If you have a wire fence, be sure that it goes *into* the ground so that no gaps invite your Min Pin to dig out. Any space that is big enough for your fist is big enough for a Min Pin to go through—fix it!

You will have to make arrangements to keep your garbage cans outside the yard fence as well—your local trash removal staff is probably not as diligent as you are in keeping your dog locked in. In fact, installing locks on yard gates is not a bad idea. That way you will not have to worry about neighbors or other people opening your gate and inadvertently letting your Min Pin out of the yard. Of course, your dog will not be out for long without supervision, but it only takes a few seconds . . .

BRINGING YOUR MIN PIN HOME

You've worked hard toward this day. You've done all your homework, and you've prepared your home and yard with all the necessary equipment and precautions. Now it is time to go and get the baby. Whether you're bringing home a puppy or an adult, it's basically the same experience. All those anxious questions come to mind. Will we like him? Will he like us? Have we done every-thing right? Will we be good parents? Be calm. Remember that what you think is anxiety might just be excitement.

Picking Up the Pup

Put the dog's crate in the car with nice, new snug-gly pads and a toy. Load up the family, and off you go!

You will spend some time at the breeder's so that the Min Pin can reacquaint himself with you and the family. Be sure that the kids are calm and quiet. The dog will probably want to initiate each of you with a face wash. Just be sure that you have been taught how to restrain the dog properly by holding the front of his front leg and shoulder.

After you finish up your paperwork with the breeder, put the dog into his safe crate, load up the family again, and off you go. Hopefully your breeder has already accustomed the dog to a crate, so there shouldn't be any crying on the way home. More likely, you might get a few barks; this is

one way the Min Pin has of communicating with you—or bossing you around. Talk about a backseat driver!

It is possible that your dog has never been in a car before. If he is securely in his crate with absorbent fleece pads, he will not get too messy if he should start to drool. With luck, the breeder will not have given the dog food or water for two hours before you pick him up. An empty stomach will lessen the chance of carsickness, but it is no guaran-tee. Sometimes a tendency toward carsickness is inherited in a dog. For the most part, dogs will out-grow the problem, especially if they are given lots of riding opportunities—in a crate with fleeces.

The procedures described here for bringing home your Min Pin are ideal conditions. This is probably not what you will want to do, especially if you are bringing home a puppy. The puppy will be so adorable that you will probably react like a caring human being and will hold him in your lap or on the seat next to you. (If you are bringing home an adult dog, you really need to have him in his crate so that he will not escape from you when

---

YOUR PUPPY'S PAPERWORK

You'll need to set up a file for your dog. Record everything that pertains to him: his breeder, the owner of record, his sire and dam, his date of birth, the date you obtained the dog, his color, his sex and his registration number. Keep your dog's health records in this file so that you will know when his shots are due and what treatments he has had over time. This is also a good place to keep a photo record of your dog, just for your fun and memories. For a list of the kinds of papers you should expect to receive with your Miniature Pinscher, see Chapter 4, "Finding Your Miniature Pinscher—Puppy, Adult or Rescue."

SET ASIDE SOME QUIET DAYS TO ACCLIMATE YOUR NEW DOG

It's important for both you and your pup to have some peaceful (at least, relatively peaceful) time together when you first start out. Under no circumstances should you bring home a new dog during a holiday. In fact, breeders usually will not let dogs go to new homes on holidays, especially Christmas or New Year's Eve—and definitely not the Fourth of July! Holidays are hectic and exciting enough, and it would not be fair to your new friend to have to take a backseat to other festivities. Do not make the mistake of giving a Min Pin as a gift unless you are absolutely, positively sure that the recipient wants one. A dog is a very big responsibility—this is one item that you do not want to have to return. If you do plan to give a dog as a holiday gift, it is best to give the recipient a snapshot of the puppy or dog and let that picture be the gift. The dog can be picked up *after* the holiday, when the household and all family members have calmed down.

you open the car door.) Be sure to have a towel with you to cover your lap and to give your dog something for snuggling. Between the towel and the warmth of your body, he will feel comforted and happy. Be sure that you are extremely careful when you get home also. Have the puppy securely in your hands before you open the car door! If you wrap him in the towel, make certain that his front legs are bound in the towel so that he can't jump out of your arms and out of the car.

Introducing Your New Pup to the Home

Take the first few days—and especially the first few moments—very easy. Give your new friend a chance to get acquainted with his new surroundings and with you. Show him where the water bowl is. Show him where you have put his bed or crate. You might put a *small* treat in the crate to make it worth exploring. (Do not use human foods as treats.) There are many different kinds of treats at the store. Remember, this is a small dog, so only give him part of a treat—he doesn't need the whole biscuit all at once. Offer him water, but do not press him to eat or drink anything immediately. There's too much more to investigate!

Now you will probably be disappointed, because the dog likely will ignore you and all the goodies you have prepared for him. He will know you are there, and he will eventually explore all your preparations, but he will be very busy doing what he has to do—get a fix on his new surroundings.

It's a good idea to take him where you expect him to do his daily toilet, whether that is outside or, in the case of apartment dwelling, perhaps a newspaper on the floor. Don't expect him to *do* anything; just give him this opportunity to look it over. On some blessed day, you will catch him doing the right thing, and then the celebration and praising can begin. We'll discuss how to housetrain your dog later in this chapter.

Give your new dog some time to get comfortable in your home. (Photograph by Mary Silfies)

Remember that schedule you prepared? Now is the time to put it into full effect. If it is time for the dog to have his quiet hour, put him in his X-pen and put the lid on. He will no doubt fuss and cry, and this is a test for you. The dog is not in any danger—he just misses his littermates or the other pals he had at the breeder's. Let him cry. Do not talk to him or be anywhere where he can see you. Just let him get it out of his system. If you absolutely can't stand it, go outside and take a walk or a drive.

You also can put a small piece of your clothing in with him to ease his loneliness. Your scent will comfort him, and he will not feel so alone. The downside of this is that if you have put a sock in with him, he will always think that your socks belong to him. A better suggestion used by many new owners is a loudly ticking clock placed *next to* or very near the bed, not in it. Heating pads or hot water bottles are *not* recommended because they can be dangerous for a dog—your new Min Pin can't control the heat being emitted.

Never, never, never go in and bail him out while he is making noise. Be sure that you appear only when the dog is quiet or asleep. He will soon associate quiet with you returning to him; it won't take long. Be brave. This is also a time of testing for who is going to be in charge—it should be you.

DAILY LIFE WITH A MIN PIN

You know something about the temperament and character of the Min Pin from previous chapters and from your other reading and research. But what about *your* temperament? Are you ready to start living with a Min Pin? Your little companion just might put your temperament to the test, so you should know a few things about yourself.

Owning a Min Pin can feel like bringing a child into the house, especially if you're a first-time owner. Your dog will want to see inside every sack and every open drawer, and he will want to know exactly what is going on in all areas that lead to the front door. If the door opens, he may well dart out, and then the chase begins unless you've done your preparations properly with a safe screen door.

When your dog goes outside, he must be on a leash or in a really secure yard because he *will* escape and will run off to investigate something. If you call your dog, he may turn around, say hello, acknowledge that he hears you and then go on about the business of checking out whatever it was that he found to be fascinating.

A Min Pin will sound an alarm if there is any new or suspicious activity. These dogs will bark; they are not quiet, passive dogs. They will even bark at butterflies or dust bunnies. And they are constantly on the go—until they settle down with a lap or a place beside you where they can snuggle.

You've been warned that Min Pins are escape artists. You need to know that they are also acrobats. A recent true story came to light. A man was on a ladder painting his living room yellow. Suddenly he felt something going up his back and onto his shoulder. It was his Min Pin! The dog had climbed the ladder and then climbed his owner's body straight uphill. Afraid that the dog would fall, the man reached up and grabbed it, but he lost his balance. The paint went flying, and he, the dog and the carpet soon had a whole gallon of yellow paint splattered all over them. No one was hurt, but what a mess!

Those first days with your Min Pin can be like one test after another. You probably have had a fantasy of a snuggly, loving little bundle of energy—when you wanted it. The Min Pin doesn't know that you actually don't want him to be energetic at all times. Of course, he will eventually tire out and get snug in his bed.

Speaking of bed, it is not a good idea to start your Min Pin off sleeping under your covers—let's get him housetrained first! Your first days, you will have to act like the Min Pin police, and you will

If your yard is not very well fenced, you must keep your Min Pin on leash when outside. (Photograph by Mary Bloom)

probably feel like a mean, rotten person. Just remember that if you can get through the first few weeks as a rigid ruler, you will have established routines that your dog will respect. This will make you both happier in the long run.

You will want the dog's confidence and affection, and he will want the same from you. Don't rush him. Don't overindulge him with treats or excessive petting. Don't expect him to play for more than a few minutes at a time. And don't *stare* at him! Watching your puppy or dog all the time will make him think he has done something wrong. He will lose his confidence and become paranoid. Just watch him out of the corner of your eye—no direct eye contact.

Remember that a puppy is used to playing with his littermates, and this includes mouthing and biting them. You will look like a good substitute at first. There is a very effective but painless way to break your puppy from biting hands, but you have to be quick. When you catch your dog biting, several times in a row you should grasp his jaw from underneath, quickly put your thumb way onto the back of the dog's tongue and then press with your thumb until it is clear that it is uncomfortable for the dog. Firmly say "no." Then release your hand and pet and love the dog. If you do this right, he will not know that your hand is causing discomfort, but he will learn not to bite down on hands that come near his face.

Think of your Min Pin as being a dog soaked in oil. He can squirt out of your arms in the blink of an eye, and he can slither off of or out of any place he doesn't want to be at that moment. Be sure that the dog is in a low-to-the-ground, safe place and is prevented from getting into danger.

CRATE-TRAINING

The merits of using a crate for your dog have been emphasized and bear repeating. A dog that is crate-trained will always feel safe and secure in his "den." This makes life so much easier for the dog if he has to go to the veterinarian or on an airplane, or if he is a show dog and must go on the road with his handler. Also, most motels will accept small dogs in crates when you go on vacation.

A new environment holds much fascination for a dog.

The crate satisfies the dog's basic animal instinct for a secure place of his own. Very, very seldom will a dog soil his crate. If that does happen, you should clean the crate immediately with soap and water and a little bleach. Be sure you are taking the dog out of his crate often enough and giving him sufficient attention. More likely than not, a dog who soils his crate simply isn't getting sufficient opportunities to use the toilet—and that means he's being neglected.

If you decide against a crate for your dog, make other provisions for his comfort. You can use a cardboard carton filled with a blanket or fleece pads. Shredded newspaper is not recommended because it is too easy for a strand of paper to get wrapped around the dog's leg and cut off circulation. You can place the carton next to your bed or anywhere in the home that is convenient, as long as there is sufficient ventilation and the location is free from dampness and drafts.

HOUSETRAINING YOUR MIN PIN

Housetraining is not about "breaking" your dog. It is really an understanding between partners: You must learn what your dog's natural requirements are, and you must teach your dog where and when you expect him to take care of these requirements. Above all, you must remember that a dog has very basic instincts, and until he knows differently, he will make his own decision about where and when he relieves himself. The dog didn't ask to be inside a house, but he will not want to soil the areas where he sleeps and eats; if he's given the opportunity, he will find a spot away from those places. Whatever method you choose, the key word is consistency. Min Pins may be a little difficult to housetrain, but persistence and positive reinforcement will pay off.

Remind yourself often that the Min Pin is a Toy breed. As a result, his bladder is small and needs to be emptied often. Another breed characteristic is that Min Pins tend to have a relatively short attention span. Together, these facts present a bit of a housetraining challenge. If you must be gone during the day, use one of the methods described here to accommodate safety and cleanliness.

One more caution that is specific to Min Pins: The dogs are very smart but very concrete in their thinking. They need to be housetrained room by room. This may not be a happy thought, but knowing it from the start will help prevent accidents and frustration in the future.

Using the X-Pen

Using the X-pen inside the house limits the area over which the dog can roam and keeps him close to his sleeping and eating areas. If you are attentive to your dog's needs, he will not ever have to soil the X-pen while in the house. If he does have to go early in his training, he will probably go to the farthest end of the pen, away from his bed. Puppies naturally make an effort to stay clean. As soon as they are up on their feet at about 3 weeks of age, they go as far away from their bed as they can to relieve themselves. From that instinct to housetraining is only a matter of time and patience.

It might get confusing if the only time your Min Pin is outside is when he is also in the X-pen. Be sure that he has had an opportunity to relieve himself *outside* the X-pen. When outside,

The X-pen outdoors should be used for recreation only, not as a place for a bathroom break. (Photograph by Mary Silfies)

use the X-pen only for recreational airing. Don't forget to secure the top, either. Of course, to guard against confusion, your Min Pin will have to learn to take care of his needs while he is on-leash. This is also a must if you are traveling with your dog.

Learning to Go On-Leash

If you are very lucky, your puppy or adult will find a great place he just can't resist and will relieve himself while you have him outside on his leash. Be happy! Be ecstatic! Make a big to-do about it, and provide a small piece of doggy treat. While you are reinforcing the concept with your dog, take him back to this same spot every time you take him out to exercise. Be sure you wait outside with him until he has done something praisewor-thy. This might mean standing in the cold, or in

the rain with an umbrella. The important point is that the dog must be given the opportunity to go where you want him to. You want him to learn to respond appropriately to whatever command you choose, such as "Be a good boy" or "Hurry up." By rewarding him with goodies or lots of praise for the right response, your dog will learn to go on command. Pretty neat, huh?

Paper-Training

Some people find that one of the joys of owning a small dog such as a Min Pin is that you actually don't have to walk him at the crack of dawn. You can train the dog to use newspapers just like a cat uses a litter box. If you decide that paper-training is the best plan for you, there are a couple ways to go about it successfully. One method is to put paper in the X-pen at the end farthest from the dog's bed and eating places, which will be close to each other at one end of the pen. It's likely that the dog will use the paper just by accident, and if you catch him as he is relieving himself on the paper, you can make a big deal of it—he will get the idea.

Another method of paper-training can be used for a dog that will not be in an X-pen. Select a small room, usually a laundry room or a small bathroom. Spread paper over the entire floor. Close the dog in the room about 30 minutes after he has eaten. Leave him there until he has taken care of his natural needs. When that is done, show your appreciation with happy words of encouragement. Gradually decrease the paper coverage until it is reduced to just one paper section.

After your Min Pin is trained to paper, it is easy to get him to go on a paper, no matter where you might be. This can be a real convenience. Don't use the color inserts, though—they are slippery and not very absorbent. In fact, if you intend to use this method, you should go to your local paper and buy roll-ends of *unprinted* newspaper. These rolls are white paper and are quite reasonable in price. If you use unprinted paper, you will not be exposing your dog to the ink, which he can absorb through the paws and which can stain the skin. It is not known whether this ink can cause illness or be poisonous to dogs, but it's best to be on the safe side.

Dealing with a Dirty Dog

At times you might come across a Miniature Pinscher that is messy in his crate. One of the more frequent reasons for Min Pins ending up in rescue operations is that they are not housetrained. This does not mean that the dog is bad; it just means either that the owners were not willing to spend the time training the dog or that they just didn't know how. Then they gave up on the dog.

If you have been working with a responsible breeder and you are getting your puppy at 12 weeks of age or so, the breeder will already have crate-trained the puppy, and you will be ahead of the game. If you are getting a rescue dog or an adult, the dedicated rescuer or the breeder who is placing the adult dog will have taken great pains to educate (or reeducate) the dog about manners.

Min Pins are naturally clean dogs and usually welcome the opportunity to stay clean. If a Min

NAMING YOUR PUPPY

Oddly enough, what you name your puppy could interfere with your training at a later date. Puppies should never be named with anything that sounds like a training word. For example, stay away from names that rhyme with *no*, *sit*, *stay*, *down* or *dog*. The old joke about naming a dog Dammit is just that—a bad joke. If your puppy is already named and you find that Beau interferes with training because of the word *no*, for example, don't despair. Just change the corrective word or the training word. For example, instead of using *no*, use *stop* instead. And, for goodness sake, don't swear around your dog. The most shaming words said to dogs are swear words.

Pin is dirty in and about his quarters, he was undoubtedly the victim of ugly circumstances during his formative learning periods. Perhaps he was purchased by people who worked long hours and was expected to wait in his crate endlessly without relief. This just doesn't work. A puppy needs to go out after every nap and meal. He can't just sit there from 7:00 A.M. to 6:00 P.M. without having to go.

If that happens, he never learns where to go; he just goes wherever he is, including in his own bed. It doesn't take much to imagine the feelings of disgrace a dog in those circumstances must experience. Eventually, however, the dog will lose his natural instinct to keep his bed clean.

Retraining these dogs takes know-how and a restructuring of their environment. The rescued dogs are put into kennel runs that are 3 feet wide by 30 feet long. Their food and water are inside a house at one end of the run. At first they defecate anywhere. When they defecate at the end of the run farthest from their house, it is an indicator that they are getting the idea of being clean. At that point, the real work can begin: housetraining. A kind of run is created inside the house, leading to a dog door that is propped open. When the dog begins to use the dog door and go outside on his own consistently, the rescuer can be fairly sure that the dog will be clean in his adopted home. Of course, the new owner will have to continue the work.

THE WELL-BEHAVED MINIATURE PINSCHER

You've brought your Miniature Pinscher home, he's housetrained and he knows his name. He even comes to you (sometimes) when you call him. Loving him and playing with him will be the focus of your energy for several months, but then he will need to learn additional manners and will need some exposure to the world outside his home.

A properly socialized and well-trained dog makes a delightful companion. A dog with poor social skills, however, is a trial for you and for the people that he meets. Although this chapter won't be able to provide everything you need to know about dog training, we'll get you and your Min Pin off on the right track.

Establishing the House Rules

Before you bring your puppy home, you should hold a conference among all members of the household. Even if you live alone, you will have to train your family and friends to the appropriate use of a totally new vocabulary. It is not okay for your neighbor to respond with "Oh, I don't mind" when your puppy jumps up on her on the side-walk. Well, you mind—or, you should—and don't forget that you are the Alpha pack leader and that you must be obeyed by the pup, friends notwithstanding.

Everyone who will come into frequent contact with the new puppy must agree to follow *your* behavior and training rules. No exceptions can be tolerated because a Min Pin is too smart. If a Min Pin sees that he can get away with something

---

DO NOT CONFUSE YOUR MIN PIN WITH YOUR PURSE

You must *not* carry your dog around. He has four feet and four perfectly good legs. If you carry him, it is degrading; it is babying him. Furthermore, he will not learn to handle conditions on the ground at his level with any sense of confidence. There's nothing worse than seeing a Min Pin shivering and cowering in his owner's arms or cringing on the ground when he sees things that are new to him. The proper Min Pin should be *intrigued* by new things, not frightened by them. Let him be the inquisitive, outgoing dog he was born to be.

when you are not around, he will lose respect for you. It's even worse if he is allowed to get away with something in your very presence! Above all, you must decide that you are willing to make a commitment to be the boss. When your Min Pin perceives that obeying you is the only proper way to behave, you'll have a dog that everyone else will want to have around because of his good behavior.

Socializing Your Puppy

Before you even think of formal training, your puppy must learn a few basics. I cannot overemphasize the importance of taking the time to socialize your young dog. Essentially, early socialization gives a Min Pin the confidence to meet life head-on, without needing to be fearful or to respond aggressively to new things. You cannot confine or isolate the Min Pin in his home for the entire time he is growing up. Early exposure to different situations, different people and different sounds and smells will make for a happy adulthood.

Informal Socializing

Start your puppy's socialization process shortly after he arrives at your home. Invite people over—start with the next-door neighbors—to meet your new puppy. It's a good idea to invite a diverse crowd. Every few days, invite someone or a small group to stop by. Be sure to include men, children and people of different races.

After your dog has had his first shots, get him out of the house. You can start by slowly putting him on-leash and letting him explore the

---

> ### THE GOLDEN RULE OF TRAINING YOUR MIN PIN
>
> Be consistent. Be consistent. Be consistent. Enforce the same rule in the same way *every time*. That is the key to success in training.

neighborhood with you. Walk different routes so that your Min Pin gets to see new things, smell new smells and maybe watch an in-line skater pass by. He'll probably want to explore everything. If you notice that something or someone scares your pup, just act nonchalant and self-assured. Speak to him in an adult (not baby-talk) voice. If you start whimpering in response or pull the dog close to you, he'll learn that the "scary" thing *is* scary.

When your Min Pin is comfortable in his local environment, try a trip to the shopping mall, where you'll find lots of people, lots of sudden noises, lots of cars and great smells! Give him little treats if he gets into exploring. Let people approach your pup, and, more importantly, let *him* take the initiative in approaching new people. They will love it, and so will he.

Another great place for socialization is convalescent hospitals. Residents and staff both usually are very happy to have a pup come to visit. (Of course, you'll have to call ahead and ask if the staff would appreciate a canine guest.) Think of all the things your pup will see: people in wheelchairs, people using walkers and using crutches, carts and many squeaky shoes. It's a great experience for everyone. Do be on the alert here and in any situation where your dog is interacting with strangers.

A young dog needs to meet lots of different people so that he learns to be a trusting adult. (Photograph by Mary Bloom)

Remember how squirmy a Min Pin can be. Rather than allow someone else to hold your dog, it's better for you to hold him up so others can touch him.

Puppy Classes

Just as important as socializing your puppy to new people, sights and sounds is socializing him to other dogs. A popular development has been the proliferation of puppy training classes that begin with puppies that are much too young for formal training. These classes are open to dogs from about 3 months to 6 months of age. Generally, the focus of puppy class is to allow the dogs to interact with one another and get used to playing nicely (remember the discussion of nipping?), and to introduce the pup to basic commands. It's never too soon to start shaping your puppy's behavior, and puppy classes will help you to do just that.

With a controlled introduction to other dogs, your Min Pin will learn to be his curious but polite self when passing another dog on the street. Does this matter? You bet. Even if your dog spends most of his time inside and is the only dog in the home, he will have to go to the veterinarian's office on occasion. Moreover, if you're thinking of showing your Min Pin, you will definitely want your dog to be comfortable with others.

Last but not least, puppy classes are a lot of fun! You'll meet other dog lovers and probably spend most of the time laughing.

Obedience Training

General agreement among long-time Min Pin fanciers is that training a Min Pin can be more than a challenge, but enormous rewards await with perseverance and patience. Part of the problem encountered in training is that a Min Pin has a very short attention span. Add that to the fact that he invariably believes that he has to personally monitor every little thing in his environment, and you can see that there is work to be done! Neither a leaf nor a dust bunny evades the attention of the ever-alert Min Pin. The best approach is to expect the unexpected. So, how do you face this challenge? (And face it you must!)

I recommend enrolling yourself and your dog (at about 6 months of age) in a good obedience class—and make sure that you practice at home.

Basic Training Classes

A basic training class is designed to train you how to train your dog. The emphasis is usually on the kinds of basic training needed to make your dog a good companion.

Playing with other puppies helps a young dog learn important interactive skills. (Photograph by Mary Bloom)

It is wise to shop around before signing up for classes. Visit the different classes, observe the trainer's methods and see how the dogs in the class seem to behave in that environment. Are they willing and happy? Is the trainer observant of breed differences and the different needs of the owners? You need to select the class that seems to fit you and your dog best.

If there are no classes in your town, ask your local recreation department for information on nearby classes.

A good class will be based on recognized behavior-management principles and will help you learn more about training your dog at home. The reward for good behavior is food! Believe me, your Min Pin will love that. Just be sure you don't put too much weight on him, which is easy to do with a Min Pin. Many behavioral clues are used in different programs of dog training, but most of them follow this sequence: state the command; place or lure the dog into the desired position; and praise and reward him. Eventually, the dog will associate the treat (reward) with the command and will begin to respond simply to the command. All dogs can be trained. If yours is not responding, it is you who needs help with your training methods.

TEACHING YOUR MIN PIN TO COME WHEN CALLED

You'll want your Min Pin to come to you every time you call him. This is extremely important for your dog's safety. If your Min Pin has decided to investigate a hornet's nest, you want him to desist and come to you *now*. Make coming to you a delight for your dog. Practice with your Min Pin on-leash. You can show him that you have a little treat, call his name and wait for him to come prancing over. If he dallies, he does not get the treat. If he responds quickly, he gets praise and the treat. When your Min Pin becomes reliable, you can slowly phase out giving a treat for every correct response. (But don't phase out the praise—you want to keep him in good form.) Do *not* call your Min Pin when you plan to do something he doesn't like. If you need to leave the park, walk over and get your dog. If you are about to trim his toenails, walk over and get your dog. Coming to your call should always be a positive experience. Why would your Min Pin come to you if you're about to put him in the wash tub? He's smart, and he'll figure out that coming is optional—or, worse yet, a bad idea.

Some of the things your young dog will learn include how to sit, how to lie down, how to stay and how to (approximately) heel by your side at your command. For example, you'll learn that to teach your dog to sit, you'll either gently push his bottom down as you say "sit," or you'll lure his nose up with a little treat and his bottom will naturally hit the ground. When he's sitting nicely, you'll praise him and give him the treat. He'll learn that it's a good idea to sit when you ask him to do so. Of course, you want an obedient dog, but you must not set your goals too high with your Min Pin on these requirements. Remember that this is a very energetic breed, and sitting still or lying down (except in a snuggle bag) can be very demanding for him. Even if he sits and stays, he will very likely be dancing with his front feet.

Be patient, and remember that this is an *introductory* class where you and he can learn the words and the ways by which to execute the commands.

You can learn together, and this is the very best bonding experience the two of you can have.

Training at Home

Obedience classes are great when learning the ropes of training your dog. But, of course, you'll need to practice at home with your Min Pin. Make a point to have at least one practice session every single day. Keep the training sessions brief—no more than ten minutes at a time—and end when your dog has responded well. Be sure to end each one on a positive note. You both want to walk away feeling good about the training session and looking forward to the next one.

What if there aren't any obedience classes near you? Well, you'll need to practice the techniques on your own. Lots of excellent training books and videos can help you learn the methods. (See the bibliography in this book for some suggested

You need to practice obedience training with your Min Pin. Here, a trainer shows how to lure a dog into a sit position (left), a down position (center) and a heeling position (right). (Photographs by Mary Bloom)

reading. You might try Andrea Arden's *Dog-Friendly Dog Training*, Howell Book House [1999], which is a fun and easy-to-read manual for the new dog owner.) Before you even start working with your dog, read a few training books in their entirety. With book in hand, put yourself through the paces until you feel comfortable enough to do it with your dog in tow. Make sure that your Min Pin is wearing a proper cloth or leather collar and leash, and be sure that you have the collar on correctly. Find a level place—pavement or grass—on which to work. If it's raining or too hot outside, practice in the garage or the family room. There's no reason a dog can't be trained inside.

Practice with your dog once or twice every day. As mentioned before, keep training sessions short so that they don't get tiresome. Always end every session on a positive note. Be sure that you both are having fun. The more you and your Min Pin enjoy training, the more you'll practice—and the better you'll get!

When your Min Pin gets the idea, he will want to learn more.

(Photograph by Jacobson Studio)

CHAPTER SIX

Keeping Your Miniature Pinscher Healthy

"Min Pins are normally healthy little dogs."
—JUANITA KEAN, BREEDER

It is true that Min Pins are in general a healthy little breed. As with most purebred dogs, responsible breeders pay close attention to maintaining good health in their dogs. Breeders are concerned about the health of their next generation, and when tests are developed for specific ailments, they tend to be guided by those test results. Breeders who are not responsible will not go to the great expense of having their dogs tested, and this is one factor that separates their dogs from those of the reputable breeder.

You should take your newly acquired Min Pin to your veterinarian soon after you get him for a checkup and an introduction. This visit gives the veterinarian a chance to become acquainted with you and your dog and to establish a record for future reference. On this visit you should bring all records given to you by the breeder, including shot records, records of any wormings and all other information about the general health of the dam and the puppies (or, of the older dog, if that is the case).

HEALTH CONCERNS FOR ALL DOGS

Each dog is subject to the hazards of the environment in which he lives. Because you are responsible for your dog, you must be alert to these hazards and do what you can to prevent your dog from being harmed by them. Sometimes prevention takes the form of medical attention; sometimes it takes the form of genetic monitoring. Whichever form it takes requires you to be proactive in safeguarding your dog.

Healthy Eyes

Because the Min Pin is overcome with curiosity about his world, he will be inclined to poke his nose into places where dirt, dust, leaves, twigs and the like can result in eye problems. The eyes should be kept clean and free of any extraneous matter; if necessary, a mild eye ointment can be applied.

Progressive Retinal Atrophy

A more difficult eye problem is progressive retinal atrophy (PRA), a disease that leads to blindness. PRA usually cannot be discovered early in a dog's life, and even after discovery, there is no treatment for it.

PRA is a progressive disease that is inherited. Unfortunately, it does not usually manifest itself until the dog is 4 or more years of age. By this time, the dog may have been bred more than once, thereby passing along the potential for the disease.

Due to late onset, testing for this disease must be done on an annual basis. A certified ophthalmologist must perform the examination, and the test results must be submitted to the Canine Eye Research Foundation (CERF) for interpretation and registration. If the eyes are clear, a certification number and date will be supplied. As mentioned, the test must be repeated every year after that date for the certification to be valid.

For PRA to be eliminated from a breed, testing of all breeding stock must be conducted and certified. If breeders then use only certified dogs *over the age of 4* in their breeding programs, the chances of a dog having or passing along PRA will decrease dramatically. New research may identify DNA markers for this disease as well, although the markers vary among breeds. If a DNA marker is found for a breed, a simple test will tell whether a given dog is a carrier or whether he will be affected with PRA later in his life.

External Parasites

External parasites, such as fleas and ticks, are more than just a nuisance: They can cause your dog great misery and disease. Make a point of keeping your Min Pin free of these nasty critters.

Coping with Fleas

A flea is a tiny insect, smaller than the head of a pin. Its claim to fame is that it *jumps* faster than you can blink. A flea lands on a host animal, bites it and takes in its blood. If there isn't a proper host animal around, the flea will use you as a substitute.

Some people believe that there are species-specific fleas: dog fleas, cat fleas, rodent fleas, and the like. Whatever the lore, a flea is a menace no matter what type it might be. Not only does it cause skin problems for your dog, but a flea also is an important part of the life cycle of the tapeworm (discussed later in this chapter). In addition, fleas of any kind can carry and transmit bubonic plague and were responsible for the Black Plague in Europe and Asia.

A daily examination of your dog will help prevent the development of a flea colony. Turn your

Keep your dog free of fleas by using a modern flea preventative. You can obtain one of these products from your veterinarian. (Photograph by Mary Bloom)

Min Pin over on his back in your lap. If fleas are present, you will see the fleas themselves or the bites and pustules on the belly and around the genitals. You can then take measures to rid your dog of the fleas.

Just in time, modern technology has brought the development of anti-flea medications and applications to prevent your dog from ever having fleas in the first place. Some of these preventatives are available over the counter; others are available only through your veterinarian. Some preventatives also repel and prevent tick infestations.

One approach is the use of monthly medication that is given by mouth. These pills come in various sizes that are appropriate for the weight of your dog—obviously, Min Pins should use the smallest dosage. Other medications are those that are applied topically, usually on the back of the neck near or at the withers. These medications and applications neutralize the flea eggs by interrupting the reproductive cycle.

Remember, the Min Pin is a housedog. If you allow him to have fleas, that means you will be exposed as well! Be sure to subject all your dog's bedding to a flea ridding and to de-flea your house, carpets and furniture.

Ticks

If you and your Min Pin live in the city, you will probably not have to worry about ticks. But what about that Sunday outing in the countryside? When your little dog goes running off through the brush and shrubs, he may well return to you with a tick. Because your Min Pin doesn't have enough coat for the tick to hide in, the tick usually will tuck itself up under the dog's arm or into some slightly longer hair around the genitals. The good news is that you can avoid the whole problem if you start a regimen of prevention for fleas with a medication that also repels ticks. If not, you might have a tick problem.

Like fleas, ticks are designed to be self-preserving. When a tick is not engorged with blood from a host, it is paper thin and small. Unless you have an educated eye, you would probably not recognize a tick in this stage. In fact, ticks are so small that they will blow in on the wind, so if there are woods nearby your home, your dog is a possible target.

The tick has a head with pinscher-like prongs; it attaches to your dog (or your leg) by using the prongs to hold on. Then it buries its head in the host and starts to feed on the host's blood. Ticks get very fat (engorged), and when they are full they drop off the host. The problem is that where they drop off (outside or inside) is where they deposit their eggs. These little ticks will lie in wait for any kind of host to come by; then they repeat the cycle.

There are two areas of concern when it comes to ticks. One is how to get the tick off your dog and destroy it before it drops off. The other is that a tick can cause a number of dangerous diseases.

- **Removing a tick.** There are various methods of getting ticks off dogs once the head is buried. Some say to hold a match to the tick to make it back out, but this can be very dangerous to your dog, even though the Min Pin usually doesn't have long hair. Other advice is to smear the tick with petroleum jelly to get it out. Yet another suggestion is to douse the tick with alcohol and hope that it will back out.

Whatever procedure you use, if the tick starts to retreat, be prepared to grab it with a tissue or some toilet paper. You might have to help it out by grabbing it with a pair of tweezers and very gently pulling until all of it—including the head—is out. Then soak the tick in alcohol for several minutes before flushing it and the tissue down the toilet. Do not flush a live tick—it will survive. Be careful not to touch the tick with your bare hands, because if you touch it you might pick up or scatter tick eggs, thereby spreading more potential ticks.

If the head of the tick is still in the dog, a hard bump and a scab will be left behind. Take your dog to the veterinarian for advice. Even if the area does not get infected, you will have to wait a long time for the bump to go away. Often a slight scar will remain.

- **Treating tick infections.** One of the most infectious diseases carried by ticks is Rocky Mountain spotted fever. Dogs that get this disease may have a temperature of 104°F or more, become listless and depressed, do not eat, have swollen lymph glands and often have difficulty breathing. Humans also can contract this disease and have symptoms of fever, headache and a rash. This disease can be diagnosed with a blood test and is treated successfully with antibiotics.

arthritis-like symptoms and lameness, fever, loss of appetite, enlarged lymph nodes and kidney disease. Lyme disease is very debilitating, and you certainly don't want your dog to contract it. Thanks to research that has developed a vaccine for dogs, a vaccine for humans has been developed recently and is expected to come into common usage.

Internal Parasites

Unfortunately, our canine friends are subject to a number of internal parasitic afflictions. Min Pins are just as susceptible as any other breed to internal parasites, and it's important for you to keep an eye out for the onset of disease.

Roundworm

Roundworms are common internal parasites, especially in puppies that are exposed to feces while in the nest. If the mother has roundworms, the eggs will be on her and will infest the puppies. Roundworms are long (about 3 to 4 inches) and white, with points at both ends. The adult female roundworm can lay up to 200,000 eggs a day, so you can see how easy it might be for your dog to become infested. Because these worms are transmitted only through feces, it is critical that your dog's areas are kept as free of stools as possible on a daily basis. It's also a good idea to keep your Min Pin from getting into the feces of other dogs.

Puppies with roundworms will not thrive but will appear thin, with a bloated belly. These worms

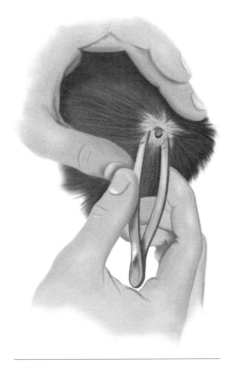

You can remove a tick using tweezers. (Illustration by Jeff Yesh)

Lyme disease is one of the most treacherous diseases transmitted by the tick. This disease is carried primarily by the deer tick, although it has now spread through hosts to other ticks as well. The disease was first identified in Lyme, Connecticut, where it got its name. Occurrence of the disease has spread to most parts of the country, and vaccinating your dog against it has become a routine preventive measure. If you take the chance of not maintaining your dog's immunization against Lyme disease and he becomes infected, you might expect could be present in egg form that's not visible to the eye. Your veterinarian will perform a stool check to discover any lurking roundworms. Subsequent treatment is rather simple, including medication and zealous cleanup after your dog.

Roundworms can be transmitted to humans as well. If they appear in your stool, get treatment immediately from your doctor. You will need to follow your doctor's directions and make serious adjustments in your sanitation practices.

Tapeworm

If your dog has "tapes," you will see small, white, rice-like segments around his anus or on his stool. The tapeworm itself can be yards long. It is acquired by consuming an intermediate host, the most common being the flea. So, once you have rid your dog and your environment of fleas, your dog is not likely to have tapeworms.

Once acquired, the tapeworm attaches itself to the intestinal wall, where it absorbs nutrients and grows by creating new segments. These segments break off as nutrients are processed through the intestine and are carried outside when the dog has a bowel movement. It may take several treatments to get the entire tapeworm out of the dog, but persistence pays off. When it's rid of the tapeworm, your dog will look and feel much healthier, with a better coat and brighter eyes.

Heartworm

Blissfully, heartworm is another disorder that can be prevented through the results of modern

A newborn pup will often have roundworms. Your new puppy will probably have been treated before you bring him home, but take him for a checkup just in case. (Photograph by Mary Bloom)

technology. Your veterinarian will start the process by performing a blood test on your dog. If your dog is deemed free of heartworm, you simply administer appropriate preventive medication so that your dog will not develop this problem. Different schedules of medication exist, and your veterinarian can advise you of the best method for a Min Pin.

Adult heartworms live in the upper heart and large arteries. They multiply to great numbers, damaging the vessel walls, impairing circulation and affecting the dog's bodily functions. Eventually, the dog will die from heart failure. Dogs become infected if bitten by a mosquito that carries the microscopic larvae of the worm. In areas where the problem is endemic, dogs are not let out at night when mosquitoes are abundant. This may be an attempt at prevention, but modern medications are a more certain approach. If your dog becomes infected, early diagnosis will lead to effective treatment.

Hookworm

The eggs of these worms are passed through the dog's feces and are often contracted from contact with stools. Sometimes the eggs hatch in the soil and attach themselves to the feet of the new host, dog or human. They then burrow into the skin and head for the intestinal tract, where they attach to the intestinal wall and suck blood. When they detach and move to a new location, the old wound continues to bleed, which produces the first warning sign: bloody diarrhea.

Children playing barefoot in dirt or sand are more likely to pick up hookworm than adults who usually keep their shoes on. Treatment is possible for humans as well as dogs, but hookworms are persistent; a series of treatments might be necessary.

Whipworm

Adult whipworms live in the large intestine and, like their cousins, feed on blood. The eggs are

Common internal parasites include (left to right) roundworm, whipworm, tapeworm and hookworm. (Illustration by Jeff Yesh)

passed in the stool and live in the soil. In infested areas, it is quite easy for your dog or *you* to pick up whipworms. Because the eggs lie in wait for years, a dog eating fresh grass might ingest the eggs. Or, your dog might pick up the eggs from a favorite toy or bone that has been in dirt where eggs lie. Humans can pick up the eggs under their fingernails if they are gardening and become infected in this way.

Symptoms include watery or bloody diarrhea and, in the dog, anemia and severe bowel problems. Because whipworms do not shed eggs continually, they are hard to detect, even with a stool sample. Several samples on succeeding days will be more likely to turn up signs. If you notice that your dog has blood in his stool or has diarrhea that doesn't pass after a day or two, get him to the veterinarian.

Infectious Diseases

You will notice that most infectious diseases are transmitted through feces, urine or saliva. Every time your dog puts his feet on the ground, no matter where that might be, he could be exposed to whatever diseases or viruses that have been deposited there by other dogs out for a pleasant stroll. Rats, mice and squirrels can also be carriers of many such diseases, including rabies. Your Min Pin would love to chase and capture a squirrel, but don't let him do it!

Most infectious diseases can be prevented by vaccinations, and immunization can be maintained through booster shots. Even though the Min Pin is a sturdy breed, he could be subject to adverse reactions to vaccinations. This is something you should discuss with your veterinarian so that the doctor can monitor your dog's reactions closely. Vaccinations in common use today combine those for distemper, leptospirosis, hepatitis, coronavirus and parvovirus. At the time these shots are given, the veterinarian also administers a vaccine to prevent kennel cough.

Puppies usually get a certain amount of immunity from their mothers, especially in the colostrum of early nursing. This immunity lasts for only a few weeks, though. If you have acquired a puppy, the breeder should have prepared a schedule

Puppies will usually have had at least one round of immunizations before they leave the breeder's facility. (Photograph by Mary Bloom)

of the appropriate puppy shots, and your puppy should already have received at least one shot—more likely, two shots—before you bring him home. Whatever schedule you have, take it to your veterinarian so that he will know exactly what immunizations your puppy has had and when follow-up shots should be given. If you do not have a shot record or any information, your vet will get you started on an appropriate routine.

Recent research has led many veterinarians to believe that dogs do not need *all* the vaccinations and booster shots that have been accepted as routine in the past. Several factors must be considered when deciding what vaccinations are right for your dog and what preventions are *not* needed. For example, if you do not live in an area where deer ticks survive, your dog will not likely need vaccinations for Lyme disease. In areas where cases of any of the infectious diseases have not been reported within the past year, prevention for those diseases is probably not necessary. You and your veterinarian should work together to formulate a prevention schedule that is appropriate for your dog. This schedule should protect your dog from diseases he is in danger of contracting, but it does not have to "protect" him from diseases that are unknown in your area.

One important word of caution: Because of the frequency of airline travel and the ease of carrying your Min Pin with you on an airplane, you must keep your veterinarian informed of different areas you have visited. Although Lyme disease could be nonexistent in the area where you live, a trip to the Northeast with your dog could put him in danger of being bitten by an infested tick.

Giardia

Giardia is a bacterial infection that lives in the mucous membrane of the small intestine. This disease is transmitted from one animal to another through drinking water contaminated with the bacteria. Most common locales of infection are standing water, lakes and streams. Unless you take your Min Pin out hunting, hiking or camping with you, he is not likely to be exposed to giardia. If your dog accompanies you on a lot of those activities, you should include a vaccine to prevent giardia in your dog's customized inoculation schedule.

One of the first symptoms of giardia is diarrhea. As you can see, any persistent evidence of diarrhea can indicate one of many possible diseases or intestinal problems and should always be a red flag about the health of your dog.

Distemper

Distemper is a highly contagious viral disease that still kills many dogs in spite of vaccinations that are usually effective. If a dog gets distemper, he will appear weak and depressed, have fever and display the most definitive symptom: discharge from the eyes and nose. He will cough, vomit and have diarrhea. The virus is spread through the saliva, urine and feces. Very little can be done to save a dog that is in full-blown distemper. Unfortunately, some dogs' immune systems are such that they contract distemper even though they have been vaccinated.

Your dog should receive his complete series of vaccinations for distemper and should have an annual booster shot to maintain protection from the disease.

Hepatitis

Canine hepatitis is not related to the kinds of hepatitis seen in humans, and it is not transmittable to humans. In dogs, a highly contagious virus attacks the liver and sometimes the kidneys. It is spread through contaminated saliva, mucus, urine or feces. Symptoms usually include vomiting, depression, abdominal pain, high fever and jaundice. The mortality rate is very high once the disease is contracted.

If your dog has undergone a regular schedule of vaccinations, he should never contract hepatitis; if he does get it, this disease is treatable if caught early.

Leptospirosis

Leptospirosis is another bacterial disease spread by the urine of wildlife or rodents. If you have mice or rats, your dog's water bowls should not be left on the ground overnight. The water will attract rodents, and if they urinate into the water, your dog faces a potential leptospirosis infection. This virus affects the kidneys, eventually causing them to fail. The bacteria can also affect humans. Symptoms include fever, loss of appetite, jaundice and probable diarrhea. Treatment for leptospirosis is available but is not very effective. Even if the dog survives, damage to the internal organs may lead to other disorders and will certainly curtail the dog's life span.

Coronavirus

Although coronavirus may be deadly in puppies, it is rarely fatal to adult dogs. Symptoms include vomiting, loss of appetite and a distinctive yellowish, watery stool that might contain mucus or blood. The virus lives in the stools and is extremely contagious enough that it can decimate an entire litter. No treatment exists for the virus, although a preventive vaccine can be given at the time of the shots for distemper, leptospirosis, hepatitis and parvovirus. If you are not planning to breed your Min Pin, it may not be necessary for your dogs to be vaccinated against coronavirus unless they will be going to dog shows, where they might be exposed to the disease. Again, talk to your veterinarian about appropriate vaccinations for your dog.

Kennel Cough

The fancy name for kennel cough is tracheobronchitis. As the name indicates, this is a respiratory infection caused by highly contagious airborne bacterial agents. The cough is associated with inflammation of the trachea, bronchi and lungs. Treatments are effective against the cough itself and can prevent pneumonia. The most common forms of the condition, bordetella and canine adenovirus, have effective vaccines for prevention. However, numerous other forms of kennel cough exist, and there is currently no vaccination available against all of them.

Rabies

Rabies has been feared by mankind for centuries. This disease is contracted only by direct infection from an already diseased animal. Until quite recently, no treatment existed to prevent death once the disease was contracted. Intra-abdominal shots then were developed as treatment, but these shots were extremely painful and risky in and of themselves. Fortunately, modern science has devoloped shots to prevent contraction of the disease after exposure; these shots are convenient and relatively painless, without serious side effects.

Once rabies is contracted, there is no cure. If you have been bitten or think you may have been scratched or bitten by a possible rabies carrier, or if you think the saliva of a possible carrier may have entered your system through a cut on your skin, get to a doctor immediately. The same advice holds for your dog, except, of course, you should take him to the veterinarian. Because all warm-blooded animals can be infected, there is a broad spectrum of danger. However, rabies is usually carried by wildlife such as bats, raccoons and skunks. It is

Talk to your veterinarian about the vaccines that are appropriate and necessary for your Min Pin. (Photograph by Mary Bloom)

transmitted by saliva through a bite or a break in the skin. From there it goes to the brain and spinal cord and travels throughout the body, affecting the entire nervous system.

Strange behaviors or behavioral changes are the first alert of a possible problem. Any behavior that is not what you might reasonably expect from an animal may be a symptom. You might see nocturnal animals roaming about during the day. If the disease is advancing, the animal's eyes will appear glazed, he will have trouble swallowing and he will drool or salivate excessively, causing the "mad dog" foaming mouth syndrome. Paralysis and convulsions develop, and a very painful death follows.

There is no reason for your dog to be endangered by rabies because very effective vaccines have been available for decades to prevent transmission of the virus. The rabies shot will be given to your dog twice in his first year. It is usually recommended that a Min Pin not receive what is called a prevaccination shot. You may have to argue with your vet about this, but the rabies shot is quite strong and the Min Pin is quite small. Most experts believe that it is best not to give a Min Pin this early shot. At about 1 year of age, your Min Pin will then have his vaccination, and this immunization must be renewed every three years.

Lyme Disease

As noted previously, Lyme disease is caused by the bite of a particular deer tick and can affect humans as well as animals. If you have been bitten, you will see a spot that resembles a target. Symptoms vary and can range from minor fever and weakness, to severe damage to internal organs, to death. Symptoms often persist, even with treatment, and can also reoccur.

If you live in an area where the disease has been reported, your veterinarian will include a series of preventive inoculations in your dog's regimen. An annual booster shot is recommended to maintain immunity. Quite recently a preventive vaccination has been developed for humans as well, to the great relief of all outdoors-people.

HEALTH CONCERNS FOR THE MINIATURE PINSCHER

A few conditions seem to appear with some regularity in the Miniature Pinscher. When looking for a dog to purchase, a buyer should inquire of the breeder whether any of these conditions has been evident in the family tree.

Demodectic Mange

Demodectic mange is a skin disease caused by a microscopic parasitic mite. Demodectic mites are found in small numbers in the hair follicles of normal dogs—dogs that do not show evidence of the mange. In dogs with evidence of mange, these mites proliferate, and large numbers inhabit the skin and hair follicles. Dogs may acquire mites from their mother two to three days after birth. Mange may involve only one or two small areas of the skin (localized mange), or large areas of the body (generalized mange).

Juvenile onset of mange occurs in dogs from 3 to 13 months old, and short-haired breeds are most commonly affected. Mange gives the dog's coat a moth-eaten appearance, usually starting around the eyes and face. Demodectic mange can

If your dog will be venturing outside, you may want to have him vaccinated against Lyme disease. (Photograph by Mary Bloom)

occur in puppies during times of stress, such as when going to a new home, at ear cropping time, or in connection with the first round of dog shots. Adult onset generally occurs in dogs more than 5 years old and is often associated with internal disease or cancer.

Localized mange is the mildest form. Usually hair loss occurs in only a few areas on the head or front legs. Most dogs with the localized form recover completely. Treatment ranges from applying ointment to the infected areas to dipping the entire dog. Your veterinarian can advise you on the proper course of action—this is not something you should try without professional supervision.

Alopecia

Quite different from mange, alopecia is a generalized loss of hair that is not caused by a parasite but is thought to be an inherited condition (a genetic anomaly). Alopecia can be very frustrating because the hair may be normal for some time and then show gradual onset of alopecia. This is different from the normal shedding of coat that occurs in the Min Pin because normal shedding is followed by hair growth/renewal. Alopecia does not self-cure with hair growth.

Alopecia is common in some short-haired breeds and has been thought to be associated with mutant coat colors such as blue and fawn. With newer tests available to the veterinary community, research on color-based mutant alopecia is opening new avenues of thought about this anomaly.

In the 1950 Miniature Pinscher breed standard revision, the blue and fawn colors were dropped because it was feared that alopecia was linked to these colors. The MPCA has been open to reviewing data on alopecia and the mutant colors for the purpose of considering reintroduction of those colors into the breed standard. At the present time, these colors remain nonadmissible in approved shows.

The degree to which a dog loses hair from alopecia ranges from minor to severe. The red dog shown here has at least the beginning of alopecia on his neck. This large bald area is likely to spread down his front and then toward the rear. (Photograph by Norma Cacka)

Epilepsy

Epilepsy is relatively common in dogs and appears in the same fashion as in humans. Nerve cells in the brain function by transmission of electrical impulses. Epilepsy is a sudden, excessive discharge of electrical energy in groups of brain cells, causing an overload that leads to a seizure. Why this spontaneous discharge occurs is not known, but in many cases this condition is hereditary.

In Min Pins, epilepsy usually becomes apparent when a dog is between 6 months and 5 years of age. Treatment for epilepsy does not cure the disease, but it controls the condition by decreasing the frequency, duration and severity of the seizure activity. In some cases, treatment eliminates the seizures altogether. Treatment is usually simple, with the administration of a daily dose of pre-scribed medication.

Many people confuse seizures with convulsions. Convulsions are not caused by electrical activity in the brain, but by a variety of other events, such as fever, poisoning or extreme stress.

Patellar Luxation (Slipping Stifles)

Patellar luxation is a dislocation of the kneecap, or patella, located in the hind leg of the dog. The kneecap may dislocate toward the inside or the outside of the leg, or may move in both directions. This can result from injury or from a congenital defect related to the ligaments. The problem also can appear in one or both hind legs.

This condition, commonly referred to as "slipping stifles," occurs in most Toy breeds and, in its mildest form, apparently causes no pain to the animal. When the stifle is "out," the dog has what is called a "hitch in his gitalong"—he will take a few steps using that foot or leg and then will lift the leg for a beat or two. Or, he might carry the affected leg for more than a few steps. Quite often, if the stifle is manually put back in place, the dog's gait appears to be totally normal.

Severe or advanced cases can cause pain with consistent limping. Treatment ranges from rest (decreasing the dog's activity for one to two weeks) to surgical intervention.

Legg's Perthes Disease

Legg's Perthes disease is often confused with congenital hip dysplasia. Although the final result may be the same—a hip joint with arthritic and osteopathic changes—the primary cause is different. Legg's Perthes disease is due to the disruption of blood supply to the ball part of the femur bone, which is the bone that meets with the pelvis to form the hip joint. The head of the femur bone eventually dies.

Problems are seen in puppies from 4 to 11 months old, usually following trauma involving the hind leg, such as falling or jumping from high places. (Min Pins are fearless and have absolutely no fear of heights!) Limping with pain is the first sign, and the dog will be reluctant to bear weight on the affected leg. The muscles eventually atrophy on the affected leg due to nonuse, and the dog will carry the leg consistently. Only an X ray can confirm the diagnosis.

When the rounded head of the femur bone wears away, the arthritic changes that result can be controlled with cortisone compounds. Restricting the dog's exercise while he is under treatment or during an attack of pain is helpful. Extreme measures involve surgery that could prolong the useful life of the dog.

Congenital Megaesophagus

Congenital megaesophagus is not visible in newborn puppies and can be verified only through autopsy. Because many young puppies die, very few are taken to the veterinarian for an autopsy, so congenital disorders can go undiscovered for generations. One such disorder is megaesophagus.

Under normal conditions, the esophagus attaches to the stomach, and food is processed into the stomach for digestion. In this developmental disorder, the esophagus somehow fails to attach to the stomach. As a result, the puppy's intake from its mother simply goes into abdominal space, and the puppy essentially starves to death. In fact, puppies dying of this disorder are described as "shriveled up."

To date, no known research is being conducted on this condition, so no evidence exists about its inheritance.

Signs of Illness

As a responsible owner you must be alert for signs of trouble, including these:

- Loss of appetite
- Sudden weight loss or gain
- Fever
- Signs of pain
- Vomiting
- Diarrhea
- Coughing
- Difficulty breathing
- Sneezing
- Increased water intake
- Increased urination or lack of control
- Excessive salivation
- Sluggishness
- Excessive scratching
- Lameness
- Seizures or convulsions

If you see evidence of illness in your Min Pin, you must get him to the veterinarian as soon as possible. The biggest clue you will have that your Min Pin is not feeling well is lack of activity. A quiet Min Pin is probably sick—check it out.

A Min Pin likes to believe that he is master of all he surveys. Indeed, when you see him standing in his yard, he looks very regal and deserving of his title as King of Toys. (Photograph by Westover)

CHAPTER SEVEN

The Care and Feeding of Your Miniature Pinscher

"There is more to raising a puppy than letting it live in your house."
—ANONYMOUS

Most breeders have specific advice on raising and feeding puppies and dogs. Norma Cacka of Bluehen Miniature Pinschers has a comprehensive packet that goes with every dog that leaves her care. Included are a pedigree, feeding instructions, shot records, veterinary referrals, training information, a supply of food and the following Pet's Bill of Rights:

1. **Pay attention to me.** We can talk and listen to each other.

2. **Be fair.** Was it my fault? Did you set limits for me?

3. **Be patient.** This is especially important when I'm young and when I grow old.

4. **Keep me healthy.** Give me proper diet, fresh water, shelter, and vet checkups.

5. **Be understanding.** I'm adapting to your world even though my nature dictates otherwise.

6. **Give me a purpose for my life.** Flatter me sometimes when I'm doing OK and sometimes just to make me feel good.

7. **Keep me safe.** I need protection from your civilization.

8. **Keep me happy.** Give me confidence and security.

9. **Tag me; I'm yours.** I can't give my phone number if I'm lost. Be sure I have an identifying tattoo or a microchip.

10. **Spay or neuter me.** I don't need to be a father or to produce a litter. I won't miss what I don't know.

11. **Have mercy.** If we have to break off our relationship, place me with someone who cares; don't just "get rid" of me. If I'm in pain and nothing can help me, don't prolong my misery.

Keep this Bill of Rights handy—it's a very smart guide for how to successfully care for your Min Pin.

Fresh water should be available at all times. (Photograph by Mary Bloom)

GOOD NUTRITION FOR THE MINIATURE PINSCHER

No matter what you feed your dog, it must be tasty, balanced and appropriate for his size. If you bought your dog from a breeder or acquired him through the Min Pin Rescue Program, you will have been given enough food for several days. This supply will be made up of the food the dog became accustomed to before you got him. Along with this food there will probably be a shopping list to tell you exactly what kind of food to buy, what kind of supplements (if any) to give and when and how much to feed. Before you do anything else, you must buy *bottled water* to give your new dog until he becomes accustomed to the water at your house—in general, bottled water should be given for at least one month. After that, gradually introduce your tap water until you have made the transition complete.

What Type of Food Is Best?

Initially, you will want to feed your dog the diet provided by the breeder. If you decide for some reason to change your puppy's diet, you *must do so gradually* over a period of seven to ten days. If you make sudden changes in diet or water, you will upset the delicate digestive system and cause diarrhea. Any change must be made by gradually adding the new food to the food to which the dog is accustomed.

- **Dry food:** A high-quality dry food (kibble) is preferred by many breeders, veterinarians and others who study canine nutrition. Kibble is convenient and easy to store, and it also gives the jaws good exercise and can help prevent plaque buildup on the teeth. When the dog is very young, you might want to add a little hot water to soften the kibble.

- **Canned food:** Many breeders will add a small (very small) bit of canned meat to their dog's kibble for palatability. A little cottage cheese can also be used with the kibble for variety.

Whether you have a puppy or an adult, feed your new Min Pin the same food that he is accustomed to eating when you first bring him home. (Photograph by Mary Bloom)

- **Supplements:** It is generally agreed that if your Min Pin is on a high-quality dry food, he will get sufficient vitamins through his diet. If you have a dog that is going through a stressful situation, such as a bitch that is in heat or caring for puppies, or if the dog is on a long show career, vitamin supplements might be a benefit. In stressful situations, a Vitamin B complex may be helpful; talk to your veterinarian about the benefits of Vitamin B for your dog and the appropriate dosage. Dogs do not manufacture and do not need Vitamin C. Other vitamin supplements can be given on an occasional schedule (once per week, for example) according to the dosage on the label for the weight of your Min Pin.

Feed Your Min Pin Dog Food, Not Food for People

Manufacturers of dog food have gone to great lengths to provide complete canine nutrition in their products. With a good-quality dog food, your Min Pin will be well fed. Do not feed your dog table scraps—and *never* feed him while you are at the table. This will teach him to beg, a very unattractive behavior. Table scraps are full of calories that your dog doesn't need, and dogs do not assimilate these types of foods. The usual results of feeding table scraps are an obese dog, a finicky eater or a dog with regular digestive upsets.

Obesity

Min Pins will eat just about everything, so you have to control your urges to give him special treats too often.

After a Min Pin has reached his full growth, his caloric needs will be quite low. Even though

Overeating will lead to obesity and its accompanying heart problems, reduced activity and downright unattractiveness. (Photograph by Matheson)

these are active dogs, they are usually "good keepers," meaning that with very little food intake they will maintain their weight quite nicely.

Finicky Eaters

If given too many treats, your dog will want treats all the time, and his regular food will lose any appeal it might have had for him when he was hungry. If your dog is perfectly healthy but starts turning his nose up at his meals, you should change your behavior because you have created a picky eater! And a picky Min Pin is in seventh heaven because he knows he's got you where he wants you—worried. What to do?

Stop giving all treats and special goodies. Present your dog with half his usual meal. Leave the dish down for ten minutes. If he doesn't eat it, pick it up and then do not offer food or treats *of any kind* until the next scheduled mealtime. (Water should always be available, of course.) Within a short time—perhaps even a day—the dog will get the message and will eat his food. Now it is time for you to retrain yourself and the other members of your household. Feed *only* when and what your dog needs. Cease and desist on the snacks. Give special treats on very rare occasions—reserve them for training or showing.

How Much to Feed

The Miniature Pinscher Club of America gives the following rules of thumb on feeding. If your dog has special needs, you might have to adjust these suggested quantities.

Best New Year Wishes

From one who is your friend sincere,
Best Wishes for a Glad New Year.

I Bring You
EVERY GOOD
BIRTHDAY WISH.

These three early-nineteenth-century postcards feature Miniature Pinschers. (Postcards courtesy of Paula Warfield)

A black-and-rust dog (top) and a red pup (right) illustrate the two major color types. (Photographs by Hofheins [top] and Westover [right])

A loyal friend and an entertaining clown, the inquisitive Min Pin is an all-season dog, whether it's dressing up for Halloween in autumn (top left), frolicking in a winter's snow (top right) or enjoying the beach in summer (bottom). (Photographs by Paula Warfield)

Miniature Pinschers are fearless, animated, intensely curious and always full of vigor. That's why they're known as the "King of Toys." (Photograph by Gail Harlan)

Growing Puppies

As puppies are growing, give about ½ ounce to 1 ounce of dry, premium dog food per pound of body weight every day. This amount is distributed throughout three to four meals, depending on the age of the puppy (give more frequent, smaller meals for the younger puppy).

Adult Dogs

Feed an adult dog about ¼ ounce to ½ ounce of dry food per pound of body weight every day. So, when they are grown, Min Pins probably only need half of what a growing puppy needs; adults also usually should be fed only one time per day. Depending on the individual dog, it may be necessary to feed your male dog slightly more than your female.

If you absolutely must succumb to the ads and are convinced that you must give your dog some canned food, the suggested ratio is ⅔ dry food and ⅓ canned.

ESSENTIAL MIN PIN CARE

Just like you, your Min Pin has emotional as well as physical needs. Caring for your dog involves more than just washing his water dish; it's about being a committed and attentive best friend.

Love and Affection

Emotional care of your Min Pin is just as important as physical care. Attention, time and devotion are as necessary to his health as any other kind of physical maintenance. Many of the things Min Pins

Your Min Pin will need lots of affection to feel a part of the family.

require are the basic things that most dogs require: your affection, your companionship and your willingness to spend quality time with your dog.

Exercise

The Min Pin was not bred to be a calm, collected, cool companion. He was bred to hunt all day and capture rodents for his master. Consequently, a Min Pin needs plenty of exercise. If you don't live in a house with a safe yard that your Min Pin can run and bound through, be sure to take him for daily long walks. This will keep him from getting bored, lethargic and overweight.

While he is running around the house, the Min Pin needs to be protected from his own innate curiosity. This breed does a lot of jumping and acrobatics, so it is easy for him to injure a limb. Try to prevent your dog from jumping off tables, counters and the like. In general, it is usually safe to let your dog jump on and off the bed or

Walking your Min Pin is important to both his physical and his mental well-being. (Photograph by Mary Bloom)

your lap, but keep an eye on other sky jumping. It is all too easy for a Min Pin to land poorly, which might lead to a broken bone, paralysis or a serious head injury.

EMERGENCY MEASURES

Sometimes unavoidable emergencies arise and threaten the health—or possibly the life—of your Min Pin. If an accident or other emergency arises, get your dog to a veterinarian if at all possible. If you cannot transport your dog immediately to a veterinarian for some reason, you will have to call upon yourself to do what is necessary under the circumstances.

It's important to recognize your limitations—you are not expected to be an expert. However, you can know how to respond in case of an emergency. Following any emergency situation, of course, you must set up a follow-up visit with your vet.

Ingesting a Foreign Object

Even if your house and all your surroundings are Min Pin–proofed—or you think they are—your Min Pin will find things so small that you can't even see them with the naked eye. He will find things you lost six months ago—that is, he will find them and then try to eat them. This will probably be your most frequent exposure to opportunities for first aid.

Look for these symptoms: Your dog will cough and choke, paw at his mouth and shake his head. Open his mouth and look inside thoroughly. Look at his tongue, both on top and underneath, at his gums and teeth, and especially at the roof of his mouth across which a piece of bone or stick can be lodged. Pull out his tongue, holding it with a handkerchief for a better grip just like your dentist does when he examines your mouth, and look down his throat.

If you see an object that isn't too deeply embedded, pull it out with your fingers or some tweezers. If you can't get the object out, off you go to the vet—provided, of course, that your dog can breathe around the object. It's amazing how blocked the airway can look and yet still allow air to pass. Remember that whatever is stuck there will be slippery from saliva. This is a good argument *against* smooth rubber balls or any other toy that is small enough to slip down the throat. Don't flirt with danger.

Handling the Injured Dog

The Min Pin's small size makes him relatively easy to handle if he becomes injured. If the dog is lying still, is unconscious or is writhing in pain, use a blanket, a coat or a large towel to cover his head before you make any attempt to pick him up. This will reduce the possibility that the dog might bite you when you handle him. Don't be distressed—a dog in pain is very likely to lash out at anything or anyone that comes near him. Yes, he may be your best bed buddy, but he is injured and frightened and is simply quite likely to bite.

A dog that has suffered a trauma, such as being hit by a car or a bicyclist, may show no signs of external injury. Nonetheless, internal injuries may be present. If the dog is weak or prostrate and has gums that are pale in color, he is likely to be hemorrhaging internally, a very serious condition. In that case, cover the dog's head and carry him to the car so that you can get him to the veterinarian. Carry him as level as possible so as not to worsen the internal injuries. Lay the dog flat on the floor of the car, covered with the blanket or another covering. If you have someone with you, have that person drive while you comfort the dog as he lies flat.

If your dog is bleeding from the nose, it may mean a head injury. If he is bleeding from the mouth, he may have cuts on his tongue or on the inside of the mouth. No matter what the case, a visit to the veterinarian is an absolute necessity.

Applying a Pressure Bandage

If your Min Pin has an open wound, but *not* a protruding bone from a compound fracture, and if the wound is bleeding freely, you must stop the flow of blood until you can get help.

Your emergency first aid kit should contain some gauze pads. Apply sterile gauze pads and put pressure on top of them. If you don't have gauze pads, use any clean cloth but *not* cotton squares or balls. Raw cotton will stick to the wound and can cause contamination. Keep applying pressure to the gauze or cloth, and get your dog to the veterinarian as soon as possible. If someone else can drive, you can administer to the dog. If you must drive, try taping the padding around the injured area—the leg, body or head, but *not* around the dog's neck!

Coping with Shock

A state of shock may follow any injury or severe fright. The dog may be completely prostrate or in a condition of nervous excitement. He probably will have a weak pulse and will be breathing in a shallow manner. The eyes will have a glassy look due to dilation (enlargement) of the pupils. Usually the gums also will be pale. These signs indicate impending failure of the circulatory system. Keep the dog as quiet as possible. Avoid noise or talk that might prompt him to try to move. In cool weather, cover him with a blanket or coat to keep his body warm and at an even temperature. Prompt veterinary care is absolutely essential because the dog will need intravenous fluids and drugs that might save his life.

Broken Bones

Min Pins are delicate—unfortunately, broken bones are not uncommon in this dog. Broken bones are usually easy to identify. The dog will show signs of intense pain and an inability to stand or use the leg or legs. In a compound fracture, the bone protrudes through the skin. Do *not* try to set any kind of a broken bone. Be aware that a fall or unfortunate leap can result in breakage of the pelvis, shoulder blade or rib cage, as well as the legs. In any case, it is important to immobilize the area as best you can and then get your dog to the veterinarian for treatment.

Sprains

Sprains and other injuries to muscles and ligaments are often hard to distinguish from broken bones. The affected area will be swollen and tender. Keep the dog quiet, immobilize the area and get him to the veterinarian.

A pulled ligament takes weeks to heal. During this time, your crate-training will pay off in a big way because the dog must be kept quite immobilized so that he doesn't reinjure the ligament. If

your Min Pin is happy in his crate, it will make his convalescence much happier for both of you.

Dislocations

Dislocations are most frequent in the hip, knee, toe and jaw. Loss of movement and swelling will occur, and your dog might hold the affected bone unnaturally. Do not attempt to replace the bone because you may cause additional damage to the surrounding tissues. Apply cold compresses to relieve pain, and, of course, take your dog for professional treatment. The sooner the joint is reset, the less severe the aftereffects will be.

Burns

Only in the most dire situation should you attempt even temporary treatment of a burn on your Min Pin. If you witness or suspect a burn from heat, fire, scalding water, acid or a lye-like substance, seek professional help immediately.

Heatstroke

When exposed to the sun or exercised hard in hot weather, your Min Pin may suffer from heatstroke. In fact, heatstroke very often occurs after a dog is left in a car with no air circulation on a hot, humid, sunny day. The temperature inside a car rises very quickly on a hot day, and in no time at all, a dog left inside can suffer enormously. Don't forget that humidity can be stifling even if there is no sunshine.

If the dog is lying down and breathing with difficulty, you have to act fast to save his life.

Reduce his body temperature by putting him in a tub partially filled with cold water, or by pouring cold water on him. You also can hold ice wrapped in a towel on his belly. Heatstroke causes severe stress, and your dog will need immediate professional care. Note: If you ever have to leave your Min Pin alone in the car on a day that is even halfway warm, find a place to park in the shade, open the windows as much as possible and don't be away more than 30 minutes. Better yet, leave your dog at home.

Always supervise a Min Pin when he's swimming, even if he's just using a baby pool. (Photograph by Mary Bloom)

Drowning

All dogs can swim, but some aren't proficient swimmers. Even the strongest swimmer can drown if he becomes exhausted. A dog may fall or get into a steep-sided pond or swimming pool where he cannot find a foothold to pull himself out.

To revive your dog, first hold him up by his hind legs to get excess water out of his lungs. Then lay him on his side, pull his tongue as far forward in his mouth as possible, and extend his head and neck forward. Then push down on his rib cage, releasing the pressure rhythmically every two seconds. Water should come out through his mouth. When water stops coming out, turn him over and repeat the process on the other side. By now your dog should be showing signs of life, coughing and scrambling trying to get up.

If your dog does not respond, try cardiopulmonary resuscitation. Before an emergency arises, ask your vet for a booklet or for instructions on how to do CPR with a Min Pin. They are sturdy, but they are small and breathing pressures must be adapted accordingly. Gently pinch his nose shut while you gently blow air into his mouth. Release his nose and perform chest compressions. Repeat this breathing in and pressing out until you get some response. As long as there is a heartbeat, there is hope. When you get response, wrap him up and take him to the veterinarian immediately. He will need professional respiratory treatment.

If you have a swimming pool, take the time to teach the dog how to swim and how to go to and use the graduated steps at the shallow end of the pool. Better yet, have someone construct a ramp with a nonslip surface that you can place at the shallow end. The ramp should extend down to the bottom of the steps, and the dog should be taught to find the ramp and walk out of the pool. Be very sure that he knows how to do this. Your Min Pin is very small, and even though he is athletic on dry land, he may be lost quickly in water.

You can't count on him being stopped by the child-proof gate once he's out, either; be sure to Min Pin–proof the gate and fence around the pool.

Poisoning

Your dog can be poisoned by anything from rodent bait to garbage. Antifreeze is a particularly dangerous toxin because it is highly poisonous and it tastes good to dogs. If your car has leaked a bit onto the garage floor, clean it up and keep your dog out.

Symptoms of poisoning include retching, pain, trembling and sometimes convulsions. Your quick response is imperative. Try to figure out what the dog got into, and call your veterinarian or the local emergency veterinarian. Another alternative is to contact the National Animal Poison Control Center at 1-888-426-4435, or call 1-900-680-0000 for professional guidance. After following instructions from one of these agencies, take your dog, the poison and a sample of the dog's vomit (if he has thrown up) to the veterinarian or an emergency clinic for treatment.

If the dog is rigid, do not administer any kind of first aid. This is usually a sign of strychnine poisoning (strychnine is commonly used in rat poison). Any form of stimulation may be harmful, so first aid may only further endanger him.

Seizures

Prior to a seizure, a dog may either run around or stand quietly. If he falls, gently restrain him with a towel or a small blanket. Do not try to muzzle him or put anything into his mouth—just keep him quiet. In fact, it is best to leave him alone—in his crate, if possible—where he will be safe.

When your dog has recovered, your veterinarian will want to examine him to try to find the cause of the seizure. If it is an inherited disorder, you should advise the breeder from whom you bought the dog. If it is indeed epilepsy, your dog can live a long, healthy life with daily medication. Seizures might also be a result of poisoning, which makes it critical that you get the dog to a vet as soon as possible following any seizure activity.

Eye Injuries

For inflammation, cuts and scratches, wash the affected eye with an eye lotion or warm tap water. Dry the eye gently with a soft cloth, and apply eye ointment from your first aid kit at least twice a day. If you haven't put a first aid kit together or if it doesn't contain a good eye ointment, it is all right to use a good ophthalmic ointment that is used for humans. If the inflammation persists for more than two days, let the veterinarian have a look.

Hazards of the Great Outdoors

Dogs love to romp outside, and we love to take them to the country. When you and your Min Pin get back to nature, however, be sure to bring your first aid kit along.

Porcupine Quills

If you're out in the country and your fearless Min Pin chases after that weird-looking rodent that turns out to be a porcupine, you're in trouble.

Porcupine quills are barbed, and they tend to work their way deeper into tissue with every slight movement. Get your dog to a veterinarian as soon as possible.

Skunks

If your Min Pin encounters a skunk and gets sprayed, you and the dog are in for it. Wash the dog's eyes well with plain warm water, and apply drops of warm olive oil to the eyes. An old "remedy" calls for a tomato juice bath. If that's all that's available, both you and your dog will need it. I recommend getting a commercial product designed to combat skunk odor.

Fishhooks

Carelessness with fishhooks is a real danger with a Min Pin around—he will find them! The hooks can get in his feet, or he might try to eat them. If your dog does try to ingest a hook and you still

Never take your Min Pin out—especially into the country—without proper identification. If your dog gets lost, he can't call you on his cell phone. (Photograph by Mary Bloom)

can see the hook in his mouth (in other words, the dog hasn't actually swallowed it), use a pair of pliers to cut off the barbed end of the hook; then pull the hook through and apply some antiseptic to the wound.

Snakes

If you are in area that has poisonous snakes, vigilance is a must. Snakes have poor vision and are really rather lazy. They'll curl up in the foliage beside a walking path and wait for something to move past them. When they sense the movement, they reach out and bite (which is why hikers need strong boots—the snake doesn't know that it's attacking a person). Even if your Min Pin doesn't immediately find and harass the snake, he is nonetheless a good target. Before you go venturing, find out how to identify any poisonous snakes in your area and how to treat a bite. If your dog is bitten by any snake, be sure to have the dog examined by a veterinarian as soon as you possibly can.

(Photograph by Mary Silfies)

CHAPTER EIGHT

Grooming Your Miniature Pinscher

"Because the Miniature Pinscher has a short coat, the grooming element is minimal."

—Miniature Pinscher Club of America

Your dog's coat is his crowning glory. Glossy hair and skin make him a more attractive companion and indicate that he is in good health.

Even though the grooming of a Min Pin is minimal, it *is* necessary to attend to the basics of good grooming: coat, nails, teeth, ears and baths. To do this, you will need very few grooming items and aids.

GROOMING FUNDAMENTALS

When you start your grooming routine, you will want to use a table so that your dog is accustomed to being examined there (your veterinarian will appreciate this, and it will make life easier for you and a judge if you decide to show your dog). Having your dog on a table also makes the grooming process a lot easier.

Lots of different types of grooming tables are for sale, but any table or bench will do as long as it has a nonslip surface, such as rubber matting. Carpeting does not work because it is very slippery to stand on and the dog will fight it. *Never ever* leave your Min Pin alone on the table, even for one second. If you turn your back, he will leap—and I do mean *leap*—and you will be on your way to see the veterinarian. The best policy is to keep one hand on the dog at all times.

In addition to a table, you'll want to have clippers, a tooth-scaler, a medium-soft brush or mitt, a chamois cloth or other soft cloth, nail clippers or a drill/file, and blunt-nosed scissors on hand.

It is wise to establish a grooming routine with your dog right from the beginning. On the very day you bring your Min Pin home, one of the ways in which you will let him know that you are in charge is to require him to sit relatively still on his table while you wipe him down with a soft cloth, look at his teeth, check out his nails and tend to his ears. Go through this routine at least daily for a few weeks; when you are finished, be sure to give him a very small special treat. Make the experience as pleasant as possible. When he seems to relax into the routine, gradually lessen the frequency, eventually ending up with his lifelong grooming schedule of twice a week.

COAT CARE

Even though it is short, the Min Pin's coat does not particularly interest fleas or general dirt. If your dog is exposed for any length of time to open

Using a table makes it easier to groom your Min Pin, but never leave him alone there. (Photograph by Mary Bloom)

ground, he will need more grooming. Overall, though, keeping your Min Pin's coat in good shape is really a breeze.

Regular Brushing

Give your dog a good, brisk brushing every few days to ensure a clean, shiny coat. A good rubbing down with your hand or a chamois should suffice to keep him in good shape. A Min Pin will undergo a rather heavy shed about twice a year. During that time, a good brushing over a period of two to three days normally pushes out most of the dead hair.

Brushing stimulates the skin, and the dogs seem to like it. After brushing, there are usually some loose hairs on the surface of the coat. That is where the soft cloth comes in—a quick rub-down will finish the job.

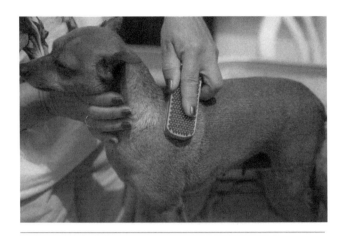

A Min Pin's coat will glisten if he's brushed regularly. (Photograph by Mary Bloom)

Baths and Skin Care

The "Saturday night rule" is aptly applied to the Min Pin. In other words, Min Pins do not need baths very often. (The only absolute exception is when a dog gets sprayed by a skunk, but let's hope that this is a rare exception.)

Actually, bathing is necessary only under extraordinary conditions. For example, if you live in the country, you might encounter some droppings from the local livestock—cattle, horses, sheep and quite often deer. Nothing can be more inviting to a

A Min Pin is a great choice if you don't enjoy bathing your dog—these dogs don't need baths very often. (Photograph by Mary Bloom)

Min Pin than a good roll in those droppings. You can visualize just how welcome the dog will be after he has enjoyed himself. In this kind of situation, a bath is *required*.

The Min Pin's coat contains natural oils that give it the luster and sheen we so admire. Bathing too often will strip away these oils, and the coat will become dry and dull. Under ordinary circumstances, a bath about once a month is more than enough to keep your Min Pin free of pests and to get rid of any grime. Every few days, it's a good idea to wipe your dog down with a damp cloth or chamois to slick off any dirt sitting on the coat. The MPCA recommends that you use a warm, damp washcloth with plain water and wipe the dog down as follows:

Begin with the face, paying particular attention to the area under the eyes, and work back toward the tail. Done every few days, this will keep your dog clean and healthy. Make sure your dog is completely dry before a trip outside.

Due to his lack of undercoat and his short hair, a Min Pin that spends much time on hard surfaces such as cement or gravel may develop calluses on his elbows and hocks. No Min Pin in his right mind would spend time on such a surface, but if it is beyond his control, this might happen. If that is the case, be sure to use a good moisturizer, such as baby oil or Vitamin E cream, on those spots regularly.

If you are going to wash your dog in the tub, or if your dog volunteers to go swimming, be sure to get all soap, saltwater and chlorine out of the coat and off the skin before drying the dog. *Never* leave your Min Pin in a crate with a dryer pointed into the crate to dry him—his skin is very sensitive to overheating, and you are likely to burn him severely. To dry him, simply rub him down with soft towels and keep him wrapped in sheepskin or in his snuggle bag with his chest well covered until he is completely dry and his skin feels to you like a normal temperature. Do not let him outside until he is dry and warm.

THE DREADED NAILS!

At least once a month, you will want to trim your dog's toenails. If you have any hesitation about doing this yourself, most professional grooming salons will take care of it for you for a small fee. Be sure to call ahead to make an appointment.

Of course, some dogs will not be as obstinate as others. It can be an enormous help if you accustom your Min Pin to having his feet handled when he is a puppy.

Nails must be kept as blunt and short as possible, which is a real chore with Min Pins because these are housedogs and don't have the opportunity to wear their nails down naturally on rough surfaces outside. Long toenails can cause

Because Min Pins chill easily, make sure your dog is towel-dried thoroughly after a bath. (Photograph by Mary Bloom)

their feet to splay out, which is unsound, unsightly and considered a very undesirable condition in the breed. It can also be painful and can lead to lameness. Neglected nails can snag on fabrics or rugs as well, and can cause injury if the nail is torn off.

When Is Trimming Necessary?

If you keep your dog's nails trimmed right from the beginning, you should never hear them go click-clack on the kitchen floor. If you hear that sound, the nails have been neglected and you must take measures to correct the situation. Nails are short enough when you don't hear that sound and when the dog is therefore standing squarely on his pads with the nails bearing none of his support.

The Technique of the Trim

The best way to trim a Min Pin's nails, whether you use a clipper or a file, is to hold the dog up in one arm while you work with the other. Hold the paw in one hand, spreading the toes out so that you can quickly come in with the other hand for the trimming. If the dog is uncooperative, wrap his body in a towel, exposing his head and one by one the foot on which you want to work.

The dog's nail is made up of a hard outer shell that is the actual nail. Inside this is softer material with a vein running through it that is called the quick. This is much the same as your fingertips: Your nails probably extend to varying lengths beyond the fleshy part of your fingertip. If you push back under the nail you will soon reach the point at which the nail is attached to your finger— that is the quick. When you push into the quick, it can hurt! It's the same for your dog.

Look at the underside of your dog's nails. The quick can be seen as the lighter center part within the circle of the nail. To shorten the nails, you must

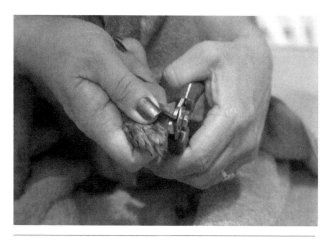

The Min Pin is small enough to tuck up under your arm, leaving both hands relatively free to do the trimming. Cut just the very tip of the nail. (Photograph by Mary Bloom)

remove the pointed portion of the hard nail itself; you want to avoid cutting the quick. It is better to remove just a tiny tip of the nail and trim again soon rather than take the chance of cutting the quick. If you do cut into the quick, the nail will bleed. Two things will happen:

1. This will hurt your dog, and he will never forget that having his nails done is painful.

2. You will need to stop the flow of blood, which can be copious.

If your dog ever tries—or even succeeds—in biting you when you cut the quick, don't be too hard on him. A dog's natural response to being hurt is to bite at the thing that hurt him—don't take it personally.

Some styptic products on the market will help stop the flow of blood. If you don't happen to have some on hand, use flour or alum. Place a bit of the substance (about ⅛ teaspoon) into your cupped palm, and press the bleeding toe into the powdery substance until the blood clots. You may have to repeat this process, but just stick with it—otherwise, you will have bloody tracks through your house.

Don't forget to trim dewclaws if they have not been removed. These nails grow above the paws on the inner leg. If the nails are unclipped, they will curl around and could cut into the skin.

The wise Min Pin owner will learn from an experienced person about nail trimming before he even begins to attempt this delicate grooming requirement. Once you have acquired the skill, you will have no further problems. If you are really hesitant or squeamish about nail trimming, let someone else do it. Be sure to do this at least once a month because your dog's toenails are like your hair and nails—they grow at a regular rate without pause (no pun intended).

GOOD TOOTH CARE

Many of the smaller breeds of dogs are prone to plaque buildup and dental problems, and the Min Pin is no exception. When your Min Pin has gotten rid of his baby teeth and has his adult teeth firmly in place, his teeth will need the same kind of preventive care recommended for you by your dentist. Well, maybe flossing isn't required, but regular brushing *is*. Depending on the amount of plaque your dog accumulates, or if you notice bad

breath and a dirty brown buildup on his teeth, he might need a full-blown tooth cleaning once in a while. Because this must be done under anesthetic, you'll want to avoid the necessity of frequent professional cleaning. Regular brushing will help to do just that.

Regular Brushing

If you start right from the beginning, you can make brushing your Min Pin's teeth a pleasant ritual that you can carry out while he is in your lap in the evening, perhaps when you're watching your favorite TV show. Initially, just run your finger along the gum line and on the outside of his teeth. When your dog is used to this kind of exam, put a little pet toothpaste on your finger and rub that on the gums and teeth.

Next comes the brush. Use a brush with soft bristles that have rounded ends. Start by brushing the outside of the front teeth in an up and down motion. Gradually extend your brushing back along the sides of the mouth until all teeth are brushed inside and out without resistance from your dog. Be persistent—and be consistent! After brushing, a *small* treat can reinforce that brushing is a positive event. This is a good time to check for loose teeth as well. If you can't get your dog to sit still for a toothbrush—and that's a small mouth to get into—just rub the teeth up and down with a cloth moistened and dipped in baking soda, salt or peroxide.

Plaque problems are especially bad in the middle-aged or older dog. If left untended, plaque buildup can lead to gum disease and loss of teeth.

Remember to give your Min Pin's teeth the same daily attention that you give to your own.

If your old dog has loose teeth, he probably has bad breath and cannot chew properly. However, bad breath can be indicative of serious systemic problems, so if you notice this (and you will), consult your vet.

Some dogs are perfectly comfortable having their teeth brushed. If you start when your Min Pin is quite young, your dog is likely to learn to cooperate. (Photograph by Mary Bloom)

Too Many Teeth!

A common problem in Toy breeds is that baby teeth often refuse to fall out or be pushed out by the incoming mature teeth. Then your puppy might have a double set of teeth. As you can imagine, it gets mighty crowded in that small jaw with all those teeth. You will notice the extra teeth as you do your brushing of the dog's teeth and gums.

If the baby teeth are not loose and do not appear as though they are going to fall out, your veterinarian will have to pull them. Do not even think of doing this yourself. If the teeth are not loose, the roots are firmly in place; pulling them will have to be done under an anesthetic or, at the very least, a heavy tranquilizer. Unless you plan to show your Min Pin, you can have extra teeth pulled at the same time the dog is spayed or neutered. This will avoid an unnecessary anesthesia.

EAR CARE

Keeping your dog's ears clean and free of debris is an important but easy aspect of good grooming.

Keeping Ears Clean

A regular part of ear care is cleaning them. Cleaning can be done with a cotton swab moistened with a cleaning solution, or it can be done with a soft, dry tissue or cotton on the end of your finger. The inside of the ear must be swabbed very carefully and without injuring the ear canal. Never put a cotton swab down into the ear canal—there's too much potential danger to the eardrum.

Ears that have been cropped or that are naturally erect are much easier to keep clean because the ear canal is open to the air. However, dogs with these types of ears will have a bit more trouble with dust-type dirt on the inner surfaces of the ear. You can clean this with alcohol, peroxide or a good commercial product applied to cotton or a cotton swab.

Because the drop ear canals do not get the air circulation of the open ear, they are more likely to collect wax and develop infections. Regular care and cleaning will prevent unwanted visits to your veterinarian. However, if you notice an unpleasant odor from the ears, take your dog to the veterinarian for an examination and treatment. Healthy ears do not have a nasty smell.

If you see scraggly or unsightly hairs around the edges of cropped ears, carefully trim them with blunt-nosed scissors. Whiskers can also be trimmed at this time. If you trim the whiskers, they must be trimmed close to the muzzle similar to a man's shave.

Cropping

If your Min Pin is not to have a show career, his breeder might not have cropped his ears. Before cropping, the ears are usually in a semi-drop position that will stay that way throughout the dog's lifetime.

Ear cropping is usually performed sometime between 12 and 16 weeks of age, when the breeder can be fairly certain that the puppy will be a show prospect. If you buy a puppy that will have his ears cropped after you acquire him, be sure to set up an agreement with the breeder that he or she will have the cropping done and will take care of the ears after the crop.

Right after the cropping is done, the pup will have to wear what is called a "rack." This rack serves two purposes: It tends to protect the ears

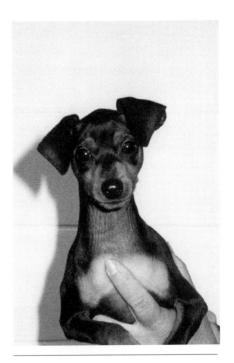

A Min Pin pup before cropping.
(Photograph by Tucker)

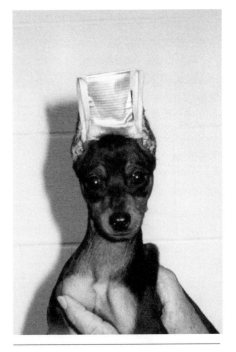

The cropped pup models his "rack."
(Photograph by Tucker)

from being bumped or roughed up by other dogs, and it helps the cartilage of the ears to "set" into the cropped form and stand upright.

Cropped ears require regular sanitary care until they heal, which is a matter of weeks. At least two or three times a week, the bandages need to be changed, with careful attention to cleansing of the cut edges. Then the tapes must be replaced carefully. You can see why this process takes experience. If you are a new Min Pin owner, you will definitely want the breeder to take care of the ears if they are cropped.

(*Photograph by Mary Bloom*)

CHAPTER NINE

Showing Your Miniature Pinscher

". . . a show-dog has to be up on its toes for a very long time . . ."
—MARY ROSLIN WILLIAMS, RENOWNED BREEDER, AUTHOR AND JUDGE

THE MIN PIN SHOW CHARACTER

Breeder and author Margaret Bagshaw shares a story about her famous Min Pin, Ch. King Eric v Konigsbach, a Best in Show dog and the ultimate in Min Pins:

King preferred men to women, but I was given due consideration as a member of the family. . . . This recalls a particular show where King was entered. We had thought his class would be called later than it was, so we had left the show grounds to have lunch. Upon our return, we saw King in the ring with a lady handler. He was not strutting as he usually did. Quickly his customary handler took over. King's appearance changed immediately and he won . . . a few words instilled confidence in King, as did applause from the ringside when he paraded. He was always fully aware of what was going on and frequently would locate the trophies on the table in the ring or in the judge's hands. Once he saw a trophy, his eyes became glued to it and he followed it wherever it was moved. King was a born showman. All miniature pinschers are not . . .

TO SHOW OR NO?

When you bought your Min Pin, did you plan to show him? Did you pay for a good specimen of the breed? Did you inquire about his potential in the show ring?

We all love our dogs and think they are the prettiest or handsomest specimens the breed has ever seen. That is our personal opinion, though. If you are going to show your dog, his success will depend on the opinion of experienced judges whose opinions may or may not be the same as yours. Judges compare each dog to the ideal, the breed standard. (This standard is presented in full in Chapter 3, "The Official Breed Standard with Interpretation.") Before you even think of showing your Min Pin, you will need to take some action:

- Compare your dog against the breed standard.

- Ask the dog's breeder and other Min Pin fanciers for their opinions.

- Decide whether you want to become involved in the time and cost of showing.

When you bought your dog, his breeder already had some idea about whether he would grow up to be of the quality required to show and become a Champion. The breeder likely kept him

Promising puppies should grow up to look like this: balanced and with a correct profile. (Photograph by Warfield)

until certain of his show potential, probably three to six months. The ears will have been cropped and cared for by the breeder, which is an advantage for you unless you have experience doing those things. Chances are that you will have maintained close contact with the breeder as you have raised your puppy and looked for answers to your questions. Check again with the breeder. Review the standard of the Min Pin with the dog's breeder, and make your decision to show or not to show. By the way, don't forget to measure your dog before you decide to show him. Be sure he is over 10 inches and under 12½ inches as measured at the withers.

SHOW-SPEAK

You will run into lots of abbreviations and terms at a show, and it will help if you have an idea of what they mean. The most important terms you will need are presented here:

AKC	American Kennel Club		MPCA	Miniature Pinscher Club of America
B&T	Black-and-tan/rust		Pull	A dog may be pulled (selected for further consideration) or pulled out of competition by the owner or agent
BBE	Bred by exhibitor			
BIS	Best in Show			
BISS	Best in Specialty Show			
BOB	Best of Breed			
BOS	Best of Opposite Sex (to Best of Breed)		RWB	Reserve Winners Bitch
			RWD	Reserve Winners Dog
BOW	Best of Winners (awarded to either the Winners Dog or the Winners Bitch, depending on the judge's opinion)		Special	A dog that has completed its Championship and is considered good enough to continue to compete
Breeder	Person who owned the dam of a litter when the litter was born		Specialty	A show in which only one breed competes
Ch.	Champion of record		UKC	United Kennel Club
CKC	Canadian Kennel Club		WB	Winners Bitch; only female to receive Championship points in that breed that day
Finish	To complete the requirements for a Championship			
Group	The seven groups of dogs specified by the AKC		WD	Winners Dog; only male to receive Championship points in that breed that day
Major	Three, four or five points			

Many of these terms are fully defined and explained along with all the dog show rules in the "Rules Applying to Dog Shows" booklet, available from the AKC in North Carolina (see Appendix A, "Organizations and More Information"). It is a good idea to familiarize yourself with this booklet's explanations of the circumstances under which a dog may be measured and under which a person can request measurement of a dog. Because Min Pins have height disqualifications, familiarity with measurement rules is very important.

HOW THE COMPETITION PROCEEDS

Some people like to start their dogs off by competing in Puppy Matches. These competitions are limited to dogs and bitches under 1 year of age. Championship points are not awarded at a Match, but it is fun to enter your dog or just visit the Match to see how it progresses. This is a great place to educate both you and your dog about show procedures. See if you can go to one of these Matches with the breeder from whom you got your dog or with another of your newfound Min Pin friends.

Your initiation into showing could come from a Puppy Match or Sweepstakes, which is usually more relaxed and less formal than a regular show. (Photograph by John Ashbey)

Whether it is a Match or a regular, licensed show, the competition usually follows the same progression. Except for the Best of Breed class, the sexes are usually divided, meaning that classes are offered separately for dogs and bitches. Dogs are entered in one (or more) of these classes: 6- to 9-month Puppy; 9- to 12-month Puppy; 12- to 18-Month; Novice; Bred By Exhibitor; American Bred; Open; or Best of Breed or Variety. The winners of each of the classes up through Open then return to the ring to compete for Winners Dog or Winners Bitch, whichever is the case. Then the dogs and bitches entered for the Best of Breed or Variety competition come into the ring, along with the Winners Dog and the Winners Bitch. The judge selects what he or she determines to be the Best of that Breed/Variety in the ring. The judge also selects between the winners for Best of Winners; the Best of Opposite Sex title then goes to the entrant that is the opposite sex to that of the Best of Breed/Variety winner.

The Winners Dog (WD) and Winners Bitch (WB) are awarded Championship points based on the number of dogs or bitches competing in the classes. If one of them defeats Champions for Best of Breed (BOB) or Best of Opposite Sex (BOS), the number of points won might be increased. It all depends on the entries at that show on that day.

• Class winners→WD or WB

• BOB competition→BOB, BOW and BOS

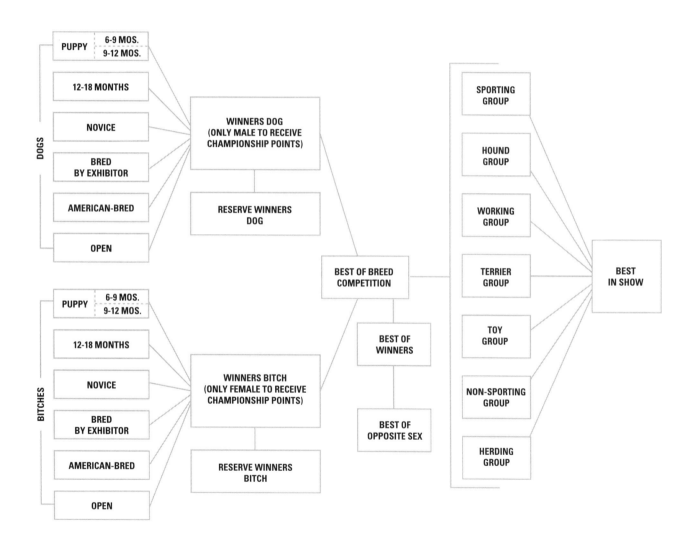

This progression goes on for every breed in which dogs are entered at the show. Each of the Breed winners then goes into its designated Group to compete. In AKC shows, there are seven Groups; the Min Pin is in the Toy Group. For the final competition, the winners of the seven Groups come into the ring to compete for Best in Show.

- BOB winners, Group competition→First through Fourth
- Group winners, Best in Show competition→BIS

What Does My Min Pin Win?

The ribbons that are awarded at licensed shows are specified by the AKC.

In each class and Group First is blue, Second is red, Third is yellow and Fourth is white.

Winners Dog and Winners Bitch receive purple ribbons.

Reserve Winners Dog and Reserve Winners Bitch receive purple-and-white ribbons.

Best of Breed receives a purple-and-gold ribbon.

Best of Winners receives a blue-and-white ribbon.

Best of Opposite Sex receives a red-and-white ribbon.

If you come out of the ring with any of these ribbons, you have been a success—congratulations! Of course, if you come out of the ring with no ribbons at all, that's okay too!

HOW TO ENTER A SHOW

Dog clubs sponsor shows, and these shows are organized by superintendents and show secretaries. Consult with your breeder for a list of superintendents or show secretaries in your area. Then call whoever is in charge of the show you want to enter, and ask for a Premium List.

This list will give you all the particulars of the show and will also include blank entry forms. The Premium List will specify the date, hours and location of the show. It also will describe any trophies offered and will state the cost for your entry. Most of the information you will need is on the entry form that you must complete and submit (with your check) to the designated address prior to the time for close of entries. After you enter a show, you'll be on that superintendent's mailing list; you can call other superintendents and ask to be put on their mailing lists, too.

Complete the entry form as follows:

1. This space will already have printed in it the name of the club hosting the show, the date of the show, the location of the show, the entry fee, where to send the entry and the closing or due date of the entry. There will be a small space for you to fill in the amount you are sending as your entry fees.

2. You will enter "Miniature Pinscher," or just "Min Pin."

3. Enter the sex of the Min Pin, either "Dog" or "Bitch," or, if you prefer, "Male" or "Female."

4. Enter here the class for which your dog is eligible: Puppy, Novice, Open and so on. Consult the AKC Rules for clear definitions of the classes and eligibility requirements or restrictions.

5. Normally, there is no class division for Min Pins. Leave this blank.

6. If entering more than one class, enter the second class here.

7. If this applies, enter the class: Novice A, Open and so on. Consult the AKC Obedience Trial Regulations for definitions of the classes and eligibility requirements or restrictions. (Also see Chapter 10, "Performance, Fun and Service.")

8. If a Junior Handler will be competing with your dog, see the back of the entry form for details needed for this competition.

9. Enter your dog's complete registered name, as shown on his registration certificate.

10. Enter your dog's registration number, as shown on his registration certificate.

11. Enter your dog's date of birth, as shown on his registration certificate.

12. Indicate the place of your dog's birth.

13. Give the name of your dog's breeder(s), as shown on his registration certificate.

14. Enter the name of your dog's sire, as shown on your dog's registration certificate.

15. Enter the name of your dog's dam, as shown on your dog's registration certificate.

16. Enter the name of your dog's owner(s), as shown on his registration certificate.

OFFICIAL CLUB ENTRY FORM

1

PLEASE TYPE OR PRINT IN BLACK INK ONLY
I ENCLOSE $ for entry fees

IMPORTANT—Read Carefully Instructions on Reverse Side Before Filling Out. Numbers in the boxes indicate sections of the instructions revelant to the information needed in that box (PLEASE PRINT)

| BREED | 2 | VARIETY [1] | SEX | 3 |

| DOG SHOW [2] [J] CLASS | 4 | CLASS [J] DIVISION Weight color etc | 5 |

| ADDITIONAL CLASSES | 6 | OBEDIENCE TRIAL CLASS | 7 | JR. SHOWMANSHIP CLASS |

NAME OF (see back) JUNIOR HANDLER (if any) 8

FULL NAME OF DOG 9

| □ AKC REG. NO □ AKC LITTER NO □ I L P NO □ FOREIGN REG. NO & COUNTRY | Enter number here 10 | DATE OF BIRTH 11 |
| PLACE OF BIRTH □ U S A □ Canada □ Foreign Do not print the above in catalog | 12 |

BREEDER 13

SIRE 14

DAM 15

ACTUAL OWNER(S) [4] 16 (Please Print)

OWNER'S ADDRESS 17

CITY _____ STATE _____ ZIP _____

NAME OF OWNER'S AGENT (IF ANY) AT THE SHOW 18

I CERTIFY that I am the actual owner of the dog, or that I am the duly authorized agent of the actual owner whose name I have entered above. In consideration of the acceptance of this entry I (we) agree to abide by the rules and regulations of The American Kennel Club in effect at the time of this show or obedience trial, and by any additional rules and regulations appearing in the premium list for this show or obedience trial or both, and further agree to be bound by the "Agreement" printed on the reverse side of this entry form. I (we) certify and represent that the dog entered is not a hazard to persons or other dogs. This entry is submitted for acceptance on the foregoing representation and agreement

SIGNATURE of owner or his agent duly authorized to make this entry 19

TELEPHONE # _____

Single copies of the latest editions of rulebooks applying to Dog Shows, Discipline, Registration, and Obedience may be obtained WITHOUT CHARGE from any Superintendent at shows where they are superintending or from THE AMERICAN KENNEL CLUB, 5800 CENTERVIEW DR #200, RALEIGH NC 27606

AGREEMENT

I (we) acknowledge that the "Rules Applying to Dog Shows", and the "Rules Applying to Registration and Discipline" and, if this entry is for an obedience trial, the "Obedience Regulations," have been made available to me (us), and that I am (we are) familiar with their contents. I (we) waive any and all claims, causes of action, I (we) might otherwise have against the AKC and any AKC approved judge, judging at this show, under AKC Rules, Regulations, and Guidelines. I (we) agree that the club holding this show or obedience trial has the right to refuse this entry for cause which the club shall deem to be sufficient. In consideration of the acceptance of this entry and of the holding of the show or obedience trial and of the opportunity to have the dog judged and to win prize money, ribbons, or trophies. I (we) agree to hold this club, its members, directors, governors, officers, agents, superintendents or show secretary and the owner or lessor of the premises and any employees of the aforementioned parties, harmless from any claim for loss or injury which may be alleged to have been caused directly or indirectly to any person or thing by the act of this dog while in or upon the show or obedience trial premises or grounds or near any entrance thereto, and I (we) personally assume all responsibility and liability for any such claim, and I (we) further agree to hold the aforementioned parties harmless from any claim for loss of this dog by disappearance, theft, death or otherwise and from any claim for damage or injury to the dog, whether such loss, disappearance theft, damage or injury, be caused or alleged to be caused by the negligence of the club or any of the parties aforementioned, or by the negligence of any other person, or any other cause or causes.

I (we) hereby assume the sole responsibility for and agree to indemnify and save the aforementioned parties harmless from any and all loss and expense (including legal fees) by reason of the liability imposed by law upon any of the aforementioned parties for damage because of bodily injuries, including death at any time resulting therefrom, sustained by any person or persons, including myself (ourselves), or on account of damage to property, arising out of or in consequence of my (our) participation in this show or obedience trial, howsoever such injuries, death or damage to property may be caused, and whether or not the same may have been caused or may be alleged to have been caused by negligence of the aforementioned parties or any of their employees or agents, or any other persons.

INSTRUCTIONS

1. (Variety) If you are entering a dog of a breed in which there are varieties for show purposes, please designate the particular variety you are entering, i.e., Cocker Spaniel (solid color black, ASCOB, parti-color), Beagles (not exceeding 13 in., over 13 in. but not exceeding 15 in.), Dachshunds (longhaired, smooth, wirehaired), Collies (rough, smooth), Bull Terriers (colored, white), Manchester Terriers (standard, toy), Chihuahuas (smooth coat, long coat), English Toy Spaniels (King Charles and Ruby, Blenheim and Prince Charles, Poodles (toy, miniature, standard).

2. The following categories of dogs may be entered and shown in Best of Breed competition. Dogs that are Champions of Record and which, according to their owners' records, have completed the requirements for a championship, but whose championships are unconfirmed. The showing of unconfirmed Champions in Best of Breed competition is limited to a period of 90 days from the date of the show where the dog completed the requirements for a championship.

3. (Dog Show class). Consult the classification in this premium list. If the dog show class in which you are entering your dog is divided, then, in addition to designating the class, specify the particular division of the class in which you are entering your dog, i.e., age division, color division, weight division.

4. A dog must be entered in the name of the person who actually owned it at the time entries for a show closed. If a registered dog has been acquired by a new owner, it must be entered in the name of its new owner in any show for which entries closed after the date of acquirement, regardless of whether the new owner has received the registration certificate indicating that the dog is recorded in his name. State on entry form whether transfer application has been mailed to AKC (For complete rule, refer to Chapter 15, Section 3).

17. Enter the owner's address, the place where you want the entry confirmation sent.

18. If the owner is not showing the dog but someone else is, enter the handler's name.

19. Sign the form and enter your telephone number.

The reverse side of the entry form contains special directions and certifications. Be sure to read the entire form, including the certification on the front.

Make a copy of both sides of the form for your records and to make it easier to complete forms in the future. Make out your check in the appropriate amount, and mail your entry with your check to the designated location within the required time frame.

HOW DOES A DOG BECOME A CHAMPION?

To become a Champion of record in the AKC registry, a dog must win a minimum of fifteen points, including two "majors" (shows of three, four, or five points). Each major must be awarded by a different judge. If your dog wins Best of Winners, he is awarded the greater number of points won by him or the winner of the other sex. For example, if your dog is WD for two points but the WB receives three points, and then your dog proceeds to win BOW, he also gets three points— a major! If by chance—and this is every breeder's dream—your dog wins the Toy Group, he receives the greatest number of points awarded that day in any of the Toy breeds. That might mean he wins four or five points. These points do not add to the points he won in the breed classes, though. The most a dog can win at any show is five points.

Every year in May, the AKC publishes a schedule of points for different areas of the country. The point schedule is based on the number of dogs or bitches shown in a specific area in the preceding year. The schedule is reproduced in the front of every show catalog. A sample looks like this:

	1 POINT		2 POINTS		3 POINTS		4 POINTS		5 POINTS	
	Dogs	Bitches	Dogs	Bitches	Dogs	Bitches	Dogs	Bitches	Dogs	Bitches
Miniature Pinschers	2	2	6	7	8	10	10	12	14	15

On his way toward Best in Show competition is Ch. Chateau Acres High and Mitey; the dog already won the Toy Group with handler Pauline Waterman. (Photograph by Gloria Knapp)

Attend Some Preview Shows

One of the best ways to prepare yourself to show your Min Pin is to attend several shows without your dog. Go along with the breeder of your dog, and watch all that goes on. Buy a catalog, and locate the ring where Min Pins will be judged. Ask questions—you will probably have many. Try not to be overwhelmed. There's a lot of noise and activity, as well as big crowds, but once you come up to the ring where the Min Pins will be shown, you will be caught up in the tension and excitement.

As you watch the classes and observe which dogs win and which ones do not, you will begin to get an idea of where your dog might fit into such a competition. Take a good look at the dogs, noting especially their side gait that will show you the hackney-like action so unique to the breed.

Be sure to watch other breeds being judged in addition to the Min Pins. Go to another ring and watch larger classes. You will notice the comings and goings of the dogs and the handlers, and pretty soon you will actually understand what you are seeing. That means you are just about ready.

When your dog has completed the requirements for a Championship, you will receive a Championship Certificate from the offices of the American Kennel Club.

PREPARING FOR YOUR SHOW DEBUT

You want to be confident the day of the show. To help alleviate the butterflies in your stomach, get yourself—and, of course, your beautiful Min Pin—ready ahead of time.

Preparing Your Min Pin

What you saw in the ring at your preview shows was an illusion. The dogs did not just happen to get into top condition. They did not wake up that morning all trimmed and glistening. They did not learn to walk on a lead and really *show* just before they entered the ring. Most important, they did not learn to allow the judge to go over them and

Ch. Marlex Mardi Gras, CD, winning a major and Best of Opposite Sex, plus finishing her Championship. (Photograph by Mary Silfies)

look into their mouths at their mother's breast. It all took *work*!

In addition to your routine grooming, you will want to cut your dog's whiskers and any scraggly hairs around his anus and at the edges of his ears to prepare for a show. If you have been rigorous about your grooming routines and schedules, you will have a cooperative dog—we hope. Min Pins do not necessarily stand still on the examination table when being judged; they are antsy. They fidget and need to watch everything the judge is doing. The place where they stand steadfast is on the floor.

Fortunately for you, a worthy Min Pin thinks he is about the size of a Great Dane, and that is how he presents himself in the ring. He will stand with his four feet firmly planted on the ground and his head held proudly on his graceful, arched neck. He will guard his little territory, a circle of ownership around him and his handler that is visible only to him.

THE BIG DAY

You've groomed your Min Pin so that he is immaculate and have practiced heeling with him so that he walks elegantly by your side. You're both ready. When you get to the show, get your catalog and locate your ring. Find a place to set up. This is where you will put your folding chair, your grooming table and your dog's crate.

You will probably go to the show with a Min Pin friend who will give you some pointers. Go to your ring and tell the ring steward that you are there. Pick up your armband, and put it on your left arm, using the rubber band provided at the ring. At the time the Min Pins are scheduled to be judged, *be ready at ringside*. When the ring steward calls for your class or calls your number, quickly enter the ring, following the ring steward's directions, with your dog at your left side.

Ring Procedures

On occasion, you and your dog may be the only entry in your class. If you are alone in your class, some judges will have you put your dog directly onto the examination table; some judges will not. Just be prepared to do what is asked. In most classes, the judge will have you (and the other competitors) walk around the ring, ending up at the examination table. If you are first in line, put your dog up on the table in the direction indicated by the judge. If you are not first in line, keep watching; when the dog ahead of you is taken off the table to be moved, that is your cue to put your dog up on the table. Pay attention. In his examination of the previous dogs, the judge will have indicated where on the table the dog should be placed and what direction he would like the dog to face.

Steady your dog as well as you can while the judge goes over him. If you have been to classes to teach you how to present your dog, this will be the time that training pays off. (Ask your breeder friend about handling classes.) After the examination, the judge will ask you to "move your dog." To be a good handler, you will have been watching exactly how the dogs move and in what direction so that you will know what the judge means.

If you are indoors, as Toy shows usually are, there will probably be mats on the floor. The common directions the judge will request are "down and back" and "triangle." If requested, take your dog directly away from the judge and directly back toward him on the mat indicated by the judge. Or, if asked for a triangle, follow the mats straight down, turn left and turn left again onto the diagonal mat. Watch the pattern of the dogs ahead of you in case your judge is using some other movement direction. Following the judge's directions

may not win the points, but it will make the judge kindly disposed toward you.

Whatever happens in the ring—whether you win or not—be sure to thank the judge, especially if you win a ribbon. If you are not in first place, be pleasant and congratulate the winner. The only way to learn how to be a gracious winner is to be a gracious loser.

Professional Handlers

You might decide that you do not want to show your dog yourself. Professionals make their livelihood training and showing dogs, and most of these professionals specialize in certain types of dogs. Again, ask your breeder about handlers who do a good job with Min Pins. Or, go to many shows

Watch the other participants to see how the judge likes the dog to be positioned on the table. (Photograph by Mary Bloom)

and watch for handlers whose manner of dealing with Min Pins or other Toy breeds particularly impresses you.

Walk past the area at the show where the handlers have their crates and pens set up. Observe how the dogs are treated by the handlers and their helpers. If you see a Min Pin or any other dog left unattended on a table or on top of a crate, do not use that handler. Min Pins cannot be left in exercise pens that do not have secured tops, either. Remember, you are the consumer. You need to be extremely fussy when looking for someone with whom you intend to entrust your dog.

When you have decided on the right handler for you, you need to find out whether that person has an opening for your dog—and you need to determine whether you and the handler have a professional rapport.

If the handler agrees to show your dog, find out about his insurance coverage and his table of fees. Determine what payment arrangements he prefers, but be cautious. Many handlers require a credit card to which they will charge all costs for the dog. This is your private determination.

The most important thing to decide is whether the dog will stay at home with you between shows or whether he will go home to the handler's kennel. The dog and handler will need some time to become accustomed to each other, so at least a short stay with the handler could be beneficial. Another thing to consider is whether to hire a male or female handler. It all depends on how your dog gets along with men or women. If he seems to be more comfortable with members of a particular sex, limit your search to handlers of that sex. If your dog does not thrive out of your presence, you will have to meet the handler at each show to deliver the dog to him there.

YOUR MIN PIN'S A CHAMPION—NOW WHAT?

After you have shown your dog (or had him shown), the natural tendency is to think that his Championship title opens the doors to breeding and "specialing." This may not be true. Yes, he has finished his title, but not all dogs are meant to be bred, and not all dogs are of special quality. This is a time for you to exercise every ounce of objectivity you have. I'll discuss breeding in more detail in Chapter 12, "To Breed or Not to Breed"; the focus here is on continuing your dog's show career.

"Specialing" Your Dog

"Specialing" refers to continuing to show your dog after he has completed his Championship. Your dog will always be entered in competition for BOB, and he will have just one chance on each day to win in the Min Pin competition. If he is a truly good dog, your intention—and that of your handler, if you have one—will be to aim for Best in Show. The dog must win both the breed competition and the Group competition to have a chance at Best in Show.

Dogs that are being specialed are top-notch dogs that are developing a record or a career in the show ring. Breed wins, Group wins and Best in

Show wins all go on record as a tribute to the quality of the dog. It's a long and expensive road, though. In a recent issue of the magazine *Top Notch Toys*, breeder/owner/handler Mrs. Judith White of Oklahoma wrote a profile of what it is like to special a Miniature Pinscher. With permission from the author and the magazine, parts of that article are presented here to give a realistic view of what it means to special your dog.

Mrs. White writes:

There are several items that I will be touching on in this article: (You)

1. *Must have the ability to present*

2. *Must have a quality dog*

3. *Must have a dog that wants to show*

4. *Must become a team*

5. *Must have available time to compete*

6. *Must have funds for advertising—little or a lot*

7. *Must know when to quit*

This information gives a good idea of what it means in time and money if you decide to special your dog yourself. If you have your dog specialed by a professional, the costs will be much higher.

1. **Must have the ability to present a dog.** *Many people think that all it takes is a good dog, and this is very far from the truth . . .*

   In Miniature Pinschers, presenting each dog is sometimes so completely different than the next one. The way you show one dog will not be correct for the next one. This is the reason

This dog, bred and shown by Mrs. White, is a Best in Show and Best in Specialty Show winner. (Photograph by Missy Yuhl)

you must spend the time to get inside the dog's head. One dog may bait beautifully, while another could care less for bait and you must "throw" them out to the end of the lead in a free stance. All of these different techniques take time, effort and a good mentor, if you can find one.

2. **Must have a quality dog.** *After you have the ability to show a dog, you must have a better-than-good dog to compete in the Group rings. For a dog to be consistent in the Groups you must have a dog that even judges who are not as familiar with our breed can say, "Hey, look at that Min Pin" and not be afraid to say it or put it up.*

A show dog has attitude. He knows that he's worth more than a quick glance.
(Photograph by Warfield)

3. ***Must have a dog that wants to show.*** *After you have the ability and the quality dog, you must have one that stands out with attitude and says to the judge, "Hey, look at me!" I have always said that a Special is the dog that goes out there and asks for the win and tells its handler and everyone around that "I am Special."*

4. ***Must become a team.*** *So now you have the ability and a quality show dog. But now you must get inside of his head, and the two of you must become a team effort. This is the difficult part of the showing adventure, and you will have arrived when you hear people comment that they love to watch that Min Pin show. He must be in a showy, King of the Hill attitude. You don't ever know what judges are sitting at ringside watching your team performance, and they might be your next Group or Best in Show judge.*

5. ***Must have available time to compete.*** *Now you have the ability, the quality showy dog and you have become a team. Now you must have the time to spend on the road showing your dog because if you are not out amongst them, you can't compete. How many weekends a month to stay in the "stats" can vary from two to four weekends a month. I don't believe that you can make a dog #1 in our breed without being able to go every weekend. But does that make a dog the "best"? No—just go as much as you can without upsetting the home fires, and enjoy the dog and its career, and don't be upset if your dog can't be #1. You know he is in your heart.*

6. ***Must have funds for advertising—little or a lot.*** *You have the ability, the quality show dog, time to show but not much money? Do it on a shoestring. You can stay in the top ten with little or no advertising. However, if you have a nice advertising budget, use it to the enhancement of the dog's career because we all know advertising works.*

7. ***Must know when to quit.*** *Now you have done all of the above; used your acquired ability to show your quality show dog with the allotted time and money you had. When do you quit showing the dog? When he tells you he is through! Too many of us are on a high with this wonderful dog, and every so often he has a bad weekend where he does not show so well, and then those weekends get closer together. Most of mine look at me in the ring with those eyes that say, "Mom, I'm not having any fun," and I think to myself, "I'm not, either." If you are a team, you both know when it's time. Don't drag your partner around the ring until people start talking about how bad he looks. Let the fancy remember your show dog in the height of his glory!*

SOME FINAL THOUGHTS

Whatever you do in showing your dog, you and he must enjoy it. Smile. Look like you're having a good time. Think of showing as going out for a nice little walk with your dog. Not only do you enjoy each other's company, but you might come home with a pretty ribbon or two!

Ch. Jay-Mac's Rambling Rose.

CHAPTER TEN

Performance, Fun and Service

*"These little dogs can do just about anything a big one can, and often a great deal better.
Even in failing they look really sharp."*
—SUZANNE HARVEY, TRAINER, EXHIBITOR AND MIN PIN DEVOTEE

You can do so many fun things with your Miniature Pinscher. In addition to showing your dog, new (and old) activities are being held all the time for dogs. Maybe you'd like to compete in obedience trials, try your hand at an agility contest or brighten the day of the elderly by visiting a nursing home with your dog. Let's examine these pastimes in more detail.

OBEDIENCE COMPETITIONS

A number of performance titles await the Miniature Pinscher. (See Appendix C, "Titles Available to the Miniature Pinscher," for a listing.) Of course, getting one—or many—of them is another story. If you see a Min Pin with a CDX (Companion Dog Excellent) or a UD (Utility Dog) after his name, you had better be duly impressed. If you see one with TD (Tracking Dog) or TDX (Tracking Dog Excellent) after his name, you are looking at a rare dog and a rare owner/ trainer.

Along with perseverance and patience, the most important characteristic required by a trainer of Min Pins is a well-developed sense of humor. Remember that these little dogs love to amuse you and when they are exposed to obedience, agility and tracking competitions, they find amusement heaven. They will find myriad ways to entertain you—most of them by doing exactly the wrong thing. This is when your sense of humor must prevail. When the dog actually does the right things, just think of the sense of achievement you will have!

The MPCA says this about Min Pins and obedience competitions:

With a knowledgeable and persistent trainer, the Miniature Pinscher can excel in obedience. Depending on their mood on any particular day, they can also leave

Ch. De-Min Diamond Danger, CDX, has beauty as well as brains, with titles on both ends of his name. He is a show Champion and also has an intermediate obedience degree. (Photograph by Mary Silfies)

onlookers and even their owner in stitches with their antics. As typical of the Min Pin personality, the more a crowd laughs, the more they will dis-perform! However, they definitely have their serious moments in the obedience ring, and many have earned the highest obedience ratings and titles possible.

You will need no reminder that the Min Pin is a small dog—you will do a lot of bending over to make contact with him for training and guidance. To get him ready to compete in obedience trials will definitely take a lot of solid preparation, but you'll both have a lot of fun along the way. And remember, the more your dog enjoys training, the more he'll look forward to it. It's a great cycle!

Whatever you do, be sure to teach your dog the right thing the first time. After a Min Pin learns something, it can be very difficult to change his mind.

In obedience competitions, the different levels of competition are known as classes. Don't confuse these classes with the puppy classes and training classes I spoke of earlier. Those classes generally teach your dog basic obedience skills and good manners. But then, these are the skills that will lead your Min Pin to success in competitive obedience classes.

The Canine Good Citizen

A great way to start in obedience is to work toward a Canine Good Citizen certificate. The Canine Good Citizen test is offered by some AKC dog clubs. The test is not really a competition against other dogs; it is a way to demonstrate that your Min Pin has developed good basic obedience skills and is calm and collected when presented with new people. A dog that has earned his certificate has proven that he's a friendly, nice dog to have around. This is a dog that you can proudly take with you as you window-shop on Main Street on Saturday afternoon.

Competitive Trials

The AKC and other dog clubs offer competitive trials in which dogs get to show off their skills. Dogs begin in the Novice class and advance through the Advanced, Open and Utility classes.

Most Min Pins do not like excessive repetitions, so the training must be kept variable and interesting. Set up some jumps around the house, and give them some leaping to do—above all else, Min Pins love to leap. (Photograph by Harvey)

Each class presents the dog with more challenging and elaborate exercises. The various exercises involved in these classes are described in the AKC's "Obedience Regulations" booklet. (Single copies of this booklet are available without charge from the American Kennel Club; see Appendix A, "Organizations and More Information," for contact information.) For example, the Open class includes jumps and retrieves. The Utility class tests the dog's

HEELING WITH A MIN PIN

Many say that the Min Pin will heel wide (away from your side) because they are afraid of being stepped on. That is a possibility, but it is more likely that in order to see you (your face) they have to get out there at an angle that gives them that view. This tendency is exacerbated if a woman wears a dress or skirt with any fullness whatsoever. When the dog looks up, all the dog will see is . . . well, you understand the problem. Pants or a straight skirt are recommended in training or competitions. Above all, do not work your dog in pants and then decide to dress up for the obedience competition! Your dog will wonder where you went, and in his efforts to find you, he will go *way* out to the side.

ability to discriminate among scents, respond to a handler's signals and to do directed jumping.

Obedience as a Way of Life

Many people's lives have revolved around doing obedience with their Min Pins. Two particular owners present their adventures here to illustrate the fact that there are no limits on where and how far you can go with your Miniature Pinscher.

Min Pins and Sue Harvey

The Harveys have been involved with Min Pins in obedience since the 1950s. Sue tells about her experiences with a few notable dogs:

It is really too bad the breed is not shown more in obedience. They are so quick to learn, eager to please, and wonderful jumpers, and they have such presence—just a joy to train and show. Over the years, each of my Min Pins has been special and unique, and very much his own little being.

My first Min Pin was 2 when he arrived. My friend Henrietta Wiltrakis had rescued two little dogs, and Cricket (Wiltrakis' Seabiscuit, UD) came to me. Because he had been badly mishandled, he was very wary, fearful of being held and dropped, and afraid of noises. It took a few months, but he gradually regained his very basic soundness. He was the steadiest, most reliable working dog I ever hope to have. He never intentionally did anything wrong—he tried so hard to please.

My next Min Pin was Wiltrakis' Sparkplug, UD. He was a puppy when I got him and was a very

different package. He was very "terrieresque"—he tracked rabbits, caught birds and was very strong-minded. Obedience was not his favorite occupation—he had more important things to do. When working in the ring, I always knew I had only a portion of the dog with me.

Wiltrakis' War Admiral was next. He never reached a height for showing in breed competition, so he came to me at age 1½. He was one of my all-time favorites—always happy, willing, straight-forward and a big show-off. Just the opposite of most dogs, he never worked as fast or as well at home as he did with an audience. He was

A family grouping of dogs owned, rescued and trained by devotee Sue Harvey. Obviously different is Afghan Sarah, CDX, with (left to right) Min Pins Wiltrakis' Mighty Ann, CD; Franciscan's Wee Willy Winkie, CDX; Wiltrakis' Peanut, UD; and Wiltrakis' Cinderella, CDX. (Photograph by Harvey)

OBEDIENCE CHALLENGES WITH THE MIN PIN

Part of obedience competition involves the dog's willingness to sit still. When you get to the point of working your dog in the Open classes, you might encounter a problem with the Long Sit and Long Down exercises. Because the owner/handler is out of sight for these exercises, the Min Pin can have difficulty with separation anxiety.

Min Pins like to have you in their sight, and when you leave, they are tempted to follow you. They also might cry throughout the exercise, or they might do something other than stay where they were left. All that can cause failure of the exercise.

This dog has mastered the Long Down, hard work for a Min Pin.

trained for utility, but I noticed he became hesitant about the bar jump. It turned out he had the start of cataracts, which made his depth perception poor, and that brought an end to his obedience career.

I immediately acquired (read: Henrietta deposited him on my doorstep) Francisco's Wee Willy Winkie. Wink was another rescue dog but had been raised with and dearly loved all children. He was the perfect dog to take to elementary schools, as he loved the kids' attention. Another one with an eyesight problem, Wink retired one leg short of his UD.

When Henrietta had to go into an assisted-care facility, I brought her five remaining dogs home. Beside the 12-year-old becoming housetrained, the 8-year-old Wiltrakis' Mighty Ann earned a CD; 4½-year-old Wiltrakis' Cinderella got her CDX; and 2½-year-old Wiltrakis' Peanut finished his UD. This

speaks well of the Min Pin's adaptability, trainability and willingness to learn at any age.

Sue continues her work with a new 2-year-old dog that has prospects for obedience and agility.

Min Pins and Gretchen Hofheins

Dominating the world of Min Pin obedience for several years has been Gretchen Hofheins of Sultans Kennels. Gretchen's dogs have won top honors at the MPCA National Specialty for several years running (see Appendix E, "Miniature Pinscher Club of America National Specialty Winners"). In 1995, at the MPCA National Specialty, Sultans walked away with the Grand Futurity winner (Puppy competition) with Ch. Sultans Sultry Temptress; High in Trial with Sultans

Lovin' Siren, UD; and Best in Junior Sweepstakes with a puppy that went on to win Best of Breed on that same day. This was truly a breeder's dream.

Gretchen states, "My breeding program consists of fairly tightly line-bred dogs. I like to do formula breeding to have a better idea of what you will get for progeny. I prefer a more elegant Min Pin. I agree with John MacNamara's philosophy of breeding dogs—get your hands on the best bitch you can."

TRACKING WITH YOUR MIN PIN

Tracking competitions are just what they sound like: a test of a dog's ability to use his nose to locate a particular item. All dogs have a very keen sense of smell, and all dogs can track." Be that as it may, most of us have images of Bloodhounds following a scent, rather than a Min Pin.

Theresa Haney of Tennessee has dispelled this notion with her work with Spice. For years, Theresa has been active in obedience with her Doberman Pinschers. Since she became involved with Min Pins five years ago, she simply assumed that she would compete in obedience with them, and so she has. She also shows her dogs in conformation. From the seven Min Pins in her life, Theresa selected Spice for tracking because she wasn't as affected by weather and terrain. With the help of hot dog pieces and very small increments in training progress, Spice is becoming a

Cinderella practices her broad jump. (Photograph by Harvey)

very good tracking dog. Theresa hopes to get her certified and tested soon, so there may be a TD for Spice in the near future. Spice's story should encourage obedience enthusiasts to push the limits with their Min Pins and consider going for the track!

GETTING INTO AGILITY

Many, many ways exist for you to have fun with your Min Pin, but the one that is most appealing is the agility competition. In a nutshell, an agility contest is like an obstacle course through which you coach your dog. The course includes tunnels, high jumps, teeter-totters and other obstacles. As the owner, your job is to lead your dog (off-leash) through the obstacles in the correct order. The dog that completes the course in the shortest amount of time wins the competition.

Contests are usually divided into levels so that more experienced teams have to work a more challenging course. The dogs are divided into groups, so the jumps are sized appropriately. (A Min Pin won't have to jump as high as a Labrador.) Agility contests are extremely entertaining, even to people not competing. The dogs have a great time, you get a bit of a workout and the two of you get an exceptional opportunity to bond.

Agility appeals to the Min Pin's natural tendency to be active and athletic. He likes leaping and racing and is a natural for agility. For all Min Pin fanciers, agility offers the opportunity to allow the dog to do all those athletic activities from which he is usually restricted. No limits here—just lots of action and lots of fun.

Nearly 100 Min Pins gained agility titles in the first years of that competition. Many of them are also Champions with obedience titles.

Min Pins are made for agility contests. (Photograph by Mary Bloom)

SERVICE

Service that dogs provide falls into a number of categories, most of which involves giving a service to impaired or disabled persons. This is right up the Min Pin's alley. These dogs are not big enough to use for sight guide dogs, but their small size and alert nature make the Min Pin perfect for many other types of service.

Hearing-Ear Dogs

Min Pins bark at the drop of a leaf, so they make excellent hearing-ear dogs for the hearing impaired. As reported in *People* magazine, soap opera star Amy Ecklund, who has been hearing impaired from the age of 6, used to rely on her two Min Pins, Eloise and Marcella, to let her know if someone was at the door. Now that Amy has had a successful surgery, the dogs are a bit confused because, according to Amy, they notice that she is telling them to be quiet a lot more!

Formally trained hearing-ear dogs will let a person know if the phone is ringing, if someone is at the door, if something is boiling on the stove, or if the alarm goes off and the like. With their acute hearing, their trainability and their desire to please,

The alert, watchful Min Pin is well-suited to serve the hearing impaired. (Photograph by Mary Bloom)

Small enough to enter tight places, Miniature Pinschers play an important role in search-and-rescue work. (Photograph by Mary Bloom)

Min Pins are excellent hearing-ear dogs. There is no better illustration than Tinker's story.

Therapy Dogs

Min Pins don't need specialized training to be good therapy dogs. When they go to convalescent hospitals, they are only too happy to leap into those available laps: people held captive by wheelchairs. They seem to sense those people who are not interested in their presence and without being told will pass by without a glance. Min Pins are just the perfect size for holding and petting. These visits mean so much to the elderly as well; many of them like holding and loving something warm and soft and alive. Many also had pets in their lives at one point, and these visits once again provide them with that bond.

If your Min Pin has a good temperament and likes people in general, he is a good candidate. If he knows a few entertaining tricks, that is helpful, too. However, for most residents in hospitals, just the presence of your dog will take them back to happy times when they had their own pets to love.

Other Service

Min Pins have been used as goodwill ambassadors in schools, scout troops, retirement communities, children's hospitals and convalescent hospitals.

Their greatest skill is their patience in being held, petted and talked to. They are small and nonthreatening, so even children who are fearful of dogs can be won over. Leave it to a Min Pin—he will head for the kids who need to get to know what a dog is all about.

In addition to being entertaining, Min Pins serve a very useful purpose as search-and-rescue dogs. They are naturally curious and so are easily trained to search and find things and people. Because they are smaller than most rescue dogs, Min Pins can get into smaller places and closer to rescue sites. Bigger is not always better!

Making her way confidently across the high beam is Ch. Goldmedal Olympia, CD, NA, TD, the only Min Pin to have these four titles. She is also an international champion, a Canine Good Citizen and a registered therapy dog (16 titles in all). She was bred, owned, trained and handled by Barbara Zagrodnick. (Photograph by Pet Portraits)

GETTING INTO THE SWING OF IT

If you have been going to organized training sessions with your Min Pin, you've probably heard about competitions held for obedience (including tracking) and agility. But how do you know where the trials and shows are, and how do you get involved? For the most part, you can rely on help from your trainer or from friends you have made in the class. Usually lists are posted for upcoming events at the class sessions, and most people who are active are aware of all the events that will be held in your area.

Before you enter any competitions, you will need to go through several weeks of training sessions (eight to twelve weeks each). At some point, you will begin to see that your dog actually knows the commands and is willing to respond favorably to them. Your trainer will give you some hints as to when you and your dog are getting ready to enter formal events. If you have stage fright, it is perfectly normal. Sometimes entering fun matches for practice will help you feel more secure. Matches are held often and are just for fun—you will not receive any qualifying points or "legs" toward your dog's title(s).

After you get through the formal Novice classes, you will feel like you've done this forever, and your experience will help newcomers. A lot of peer support is associated with these events, and you and your dog will have the cheers and

Ch. Goldmedal Tax Exemption, Am/Can CD, NA/JAS, soars over the high jump and through the tire jump! This dog was bred, owned, trained and handled by Barbara Zagrodnick. (Photographs by Pet Portraits)

encouragement of your classmates as well as your competitors in the ring. Everyone is in the sport for the fun of being out there with their dog, and for the most part a relaxed, fun atmosphere surrounds the performance rings.

Trial Schedules

Dog shows, obedience trials and agility events are supervised usually by a show or trial secretary, or a professional superintendent. Superintendents are approved by the American Kennel Club and organize many of the events in the country.

Once you enter a show under a superintendent's supervision, your name will go on his mailing list and you will automatically receive Premium Lists for all his shows. For the names of superintendents in your area or the area in which you are likely to make entries, call the American Kennel Club (see Appendix A, "Organizations and More Information"). All you have to do then is call the superintendent or show secretary and ask for Premium Lists for upcoming activities.

Entering a Competition

Chapter 9, "Showing Your Miniature Pinscher," gives full instructions on how to fill out entry forms; you would follow the same procedures to enter obedience trials and agility events. All you have to do is complete the entry form and send it with the appropriate fees to the superintendent or show/trial secretary whose name and address appear on the entry form and in the Premium List.

The Big Event

About a week before the event, you'll receive a judging program. This program specifies the time of judging for all classes or breeds and tells which ring the class will be in and who the judge will be. You will get your exhibitor's ticket along with the judging program, and that will tell you your dog's armband or identification number, the number by which he will be identified in his class.

No matter what number you have in relationship to the class numbers, you must plan to be at the show one hour *before* the scheduled time of your dog's class. Even if your class has dogs numbered 12 to 55 and your dog's number is 42, that does not necessarily mean that you have extra time. Too many times many of the dogs are absent and—guess what?—your dog will be the third or fourth dog into the ring! You had better be there and ready, or you'll miss your chance—judges are not required to wait for dogs, and you might be marked absent.

When you get to the show, find your ring and check in with the ring steward, who will give you your armband with your dog's identification number. This armband goes on your left arm, anchored by a rubber band that the ring steward will give you. All you have to do then is wait your turn and have fun and success with your dog.

Whether you decide you want to get involved with performance events, just have fun with your dog or work in the service arena, do it with flair—and do it with a Min Pin!

CHAPTER ELEVEN

Headliners

To any dog lover, it is extremely difficult to select a handful of dogs to feature in a book of this nature. There are so many exceptional Min Pins—in conformation, in obedience and in life! But unfortunately, there just isn't room to talk about them all. It's true that all the dogs discussed in this chapter are exceptional, but there are also many outstanding dogs not included.

GREAT MIN PINS IN THE OBEDIENCE RING

As you know from the previous chapter, the Miniature Pinscher is a snappy worker in obedience. A few of the standouts are featured here.

Sultans Lovin' Siren

An undeniable obedience star in the 1990s has been the black-and-rust Sultans Lovin' Siren, UD, CGC. Siren won High in Trial at the MPCA National Specialty in 1995, 1998 and 1999. Siren carries on the heritage of her dam, Der Stutz Zelda Zing, UD.

Sultans Lovin' Siren. (Photograph by Glazbrook)

Zelda Zing. (Photograph by Gretchen S. Hofheins)

Zelda Zing

Zelda Zing, UD, was High in Trial at the National in 1989 and 1993. Obedience competitions have been offered at the National only since the late 1980s, so you can see that these winners—owned, trained and handled by Gretchen Hofheins—are stars.

Korona's Black Beard, CDX

A very special Obedience Min Pin is Korona's Black Beard, CDX, the number one Miniature Pinscher and number fifteen Toy dog in obedience in 1991.

GREAT MIN PINS IN THE SHOW RING

The Min Pin continued to improve and thrive during the decade of the 1990s. While there are virtually hundreds of Min Pins winning and developing records all over the country, it is not possible to include them all. Certainly next week there will be a new Best in Show Min Pin setting yet another record.

Korona's Black Beard ("Bogie"). (Photograph by Booth)

The evolution of the breed over time has always depended on dedicated breeders and the dogs they breed that have excellent breed character. When breed quality continues to emerge from one generation after another, these producers are the true stars, as well as the icebreakers that pave the way for more exposure and prestige for the breed. A few of these winners and stars are presented here. Also refer to Chapter 2, "The Miniature Pinscher Heritage," for a look at some of the prominent winners that have had a major impact on the breed.

Ch. Shorewood's Chase the Wind

Ch. Shorewood's Chase the Wind is at the top of the show dog game. You can see the depth of devotion given by this top-winning Min Pin to his breeder and handler, Earl Shore.

Ch. Pevensey's Bits N Pieces

On the cusp of the 1990s was the top winner, Ch. Pevensey's Bits N Pieces. Bits N Pieces was a Top Ten Min Pin in 1991.

Ch. Larcons Half-Pint O'Cider, CD, CGC

Those breeders with fortitude have dedicated themselves to showing their Min Pins with uncropped ears, and they are winning!

With his natural and erect ears, it's easy to see why the Min Pin was once called the Reh Pinscher. The resemblance to a tiny red deer is

Ch. Shorewood's Chase the Wind.

Ch. Pevensey's Bits N Pieces. (Photograph by Chuck Tatham)

Ch. Larcons Half-Pint O'Cider, CD, CGC. (Photograph by Candids by Connie)

remarkable. The young Ch. Larcons Half-Pint O'Cider, CD, CGC has performed well in both conformation and obedience.

Ch. Mercer's Desert Dust Devil

One of the most prominent headliners was Ch. Mercer's Desert Dust Devil, who was Best of Breed at the MPCA National Specialty a record six times.

Roadshow Steppin' on the Edge

The MPCA National Specialty winner in 1999 was a handsome red, Roadshow Steppin' on the Edge.

Ch. Mercer's Desert Dust Devil.

Ch. Roadshow Steppin' on the Edge. (Photograph courtesy of Paula Gibson)

Ch. Charkara March-On Kall Me Wow. (Photograph by Kohler)

Ch. March-On Charkara Make a Deal

The Stud Dog class at a specialty show is judged on the basis of how well the stud dog has been able to reproduce himself and his qualities. To win at a National Specialty is extraordinary, which was exactly what Best in Specialty Show winner Ch. March-On Charkara Make a Deal did in June 1999.

Very often, top winners will produce top winners, as can be seen in the look-alike nature of the stud dog and his get at the 1999 National Specialty. A series of generations of winners usually come from a few kennels, and the March-On Charkara kennel is no exception.

Ch. March-On Charkara Smart Money

Ch. March-On Charkara Smart Money, a multiple Group winner, is shown here being rewarded for his looks and style by the incomparable judge, Mrs. Anne Rogers Clark.

Ch. Charkara March-On Kall Me Wow

Making the point of quality begets quality, this youngster, Ch. Charkara March-On Kall Me Wow, was the winner of the 1998 National Specialty Futurity and is an offspring of Ch. March-On Charkara Smart Money. Wow also has multiple Best of Breed wins and many Group placings.

Ch. March-On Charkara Make a Deal (left) is shown here with his "get," Ch. Charkara March-On Play the Red (center) and Charkara March-On Payback (right).

Ch. March-On Charkara Smart Money. (Photograph by Rich Bergman)

Ch. Little Kings Fire Walker. (Photograph by Downey Dog Show Photography)

Ch. Dynasty's Own Twist ("Perry"). (Photograph by Earl Graham Studio)

Ch. Dynasty's Speaking of Him ("Harry"), shown here as a very young puppy, winning under the author. (Photograph by Bonnie Gray Photography)

Ch. Dynasty's Own Twist and Ch. Dynasty's Speaking of Him

Succeeding generations of winners are always pleasing to breeders. Another breeder's delight is to produce a litter full of top winners. The litter brothers from Dynasty, nicknamed Harry and Perry, are consistent top winners, and Harry maintains his position as Number One Miniature Pinscher in the country. Perry is known for his exquisite hackney-like gait.

Ch. Little Kings FireWalker

Good things sometimes come in pairs, if not batches. Littermates of quality are often found in the show ring winning top honors. Ch. Little Kings Be Bop A Lula and her littermate Ch. Little Kings Fire Walker prove the point. Lula has been a consistent winner, and Fire Walker was a Top Ten Min Pin in 1997.

(Photograph by Mary Bloom)

CHAPTER TWELVE

To Breed or Not to Breed

"I always breed for temperament first and foremost because if I can't stand the dog, how do I think someone else could?"
—BILLIE JEAN SHULER, BREEDER

The Miniature Pinscher Club of America clearly states its goal in the Constitution and bylaws: "to encourage and promote quality in the breeding of purebred Miniature Pinschers and to do all possible to bring their natural qualities to perfection."

This next section focuses primarily on the bitch and responsibilities related to her. Breeding your male also has responsibilities, which will be addressed later.

BREEDER RESPONSIBILITIES

The American Kennel Club imposes a responsibility on every breeder to keep full and accurate records of all litters and their disposition. In fact, the AKC has the right to inspect your records, your facilities and the proper identification of your dogs at any time.

Breeders have a responsibility to the breed itself. It is necessary to have a thorough knowledge of the breed and the breed standard, as well as the ancestry of the bitch and the stud dog. Personal knowledge of both animals is preferred because breeding any animal with poor temperament is absolutely irresponsible.

There's no money to be made in breeding Miniature Pinschers. In fact, breeding them is an expensive labor of love, with costs that include the breeding, ear cropping, and veterinary care. Min Pins are usually good free-whelpers, but on some occasions a Caesarian operation, or C-section, is necessary to save the bitch and the puppies.

Breeders also have a responsibility to the puppies, to care for them and raise them properly, and to find homes for them for which they are best suited and where they will be happiest. It is like finding homes for your children, if you were required to do that.

Unless you're ready to care for a litter of puppies for their entire lives, you should think twice about breeding your dog. (Photograph by Mary Bloom)

BEING A RESPONSIBLE BREEDER

If you intend to be a responsible breeder, you need to talk to several other Min Pin breeders to find out what is involved that is specific to Min Pins, such as ear cropping. Enlist the help of the breeder from whom you got your dog or bitch. Together, you will go over the pedigrees of the bitch and the dog or dogs you are thinking of breeding. You will think ahead to the estimated time of whelping and the three months that follow to see whether your time and energy will be free to focus on those puppies and their proper upbringing.

Are you prepared to devote your time to socializing and training your puppies? Are you prepared to meet the demands of puppy buyers who want guarantees of health and soundness? Are you prepared to take back dogs that do not work out in their new homes? Are you prepared to pay for spaying or neutering those puppies that are of pet quality and not to be used for breeding? If your answer is "No" to any of these questions, *do not breed your Min Pin.*

Do you have sufficient space and equipment to care for the puppies: pens with covers, crates and exercise space? Do you know how to care for ears that have been cropped? Do you know how to cut toenails? Do you know how to socialize a puppy? Do you know how to train a puppy to walk on a lead? Do you know how to raise a puppy so that he has an absolutely arrogant attitude and can be and act like a Min Pin? If your answer is "No" to any of these questions, *do not breed your Min Pin.*

A truly responsible breeder will be prepared to keep all the puppies, if that is necessary.

After all factors have been considered, if you have any serious doubts about the breeding or about the care and welfare of the bitch and the puppies, you, as a responsible breeder, will decide not to breed.

Sometimes the breeder from whom you got your Min Pin might request or be willing to take your dog or bitch back specifically for the purpose of breeding. If that is the case, be certain that you have a signed contract that fully outlines all the terms of such an agreement. An oral agreement simply doesn't count; you must have a written contract, or you are courting trouble. It doesn't matter that the other person is your closest friend or even your mother—get a contract!

THE BROOD BITCH

As a Toy breed, the Min Pin bitch will come into "heat" or "season" (breeding time) when she's about 4 to 6 months old. This is much too early to breed her! As a rule of thumb, no Min Pin should be bred until the dog has matured, which is between 15 and 18 months of age. By that time, you can make a reasonable evaluation of whether that Min Pin should be bred at all.

After the first breeding, a bitch can be bred again the following season if she is in good condition and if you have the stamina for another litter of puppies. Sometimes having a litter will delay the normal cycle so that she might not come into season again until six to eight months after the previous puppies are weaned. Remember that whelping and raising puppies is quite a drain on the bitch, so don't be in a hurry to breed her too soon. Her

body will need time to restore nutrient reserves and to allow the reproductive system to come back to normal. A litter every other season is plenty, and most bitches are only bred two to three times in their lifetimes.

Before the Min Pin bitch is to be bred, she must be in good health, free from any disease and free from internal and external parasites. Her immunizations must be up to date, and she must also be in good physical condition. The bitch's condition is the most important factor in the strength and health of your puppies, so it must be absolutely top-flight.

THE BREEDING

Choose the stud dog well in advance, and make clear arrangements with his owner about the cost of the breeding and how and where your bitch will be kept during the breeding time.

If this is to be a breeding using frozen sperm, consult the AKC for instructions and regulations regarding this type of breeding. If it will be necessary to ship your dog to the stud dog, contact the airline of your choice well in advance because there are certain requirements for air-shipping dogs. It may be more cost-effective for you to fly to the stud dog's location, carrying your bitch onboard the aircraft in a proper carrier. It also will be more pleasant for the dog to have you with her during the flight.

Bitches are usually in season for about three weeks. Breeding times in the cycle vary, but at some time between nine to fourteen days is usually about right. The bitch will let the stud dog know when she is ready. If she seems reluctant, have your veterinarian perform a vaginal swab to determine the correct breeding time.

The Signs of Pregnancy

Bitches go through varying symptoms of pregnancy. In fact, some will show all the symptoms but will not even be pregnant. This is called a false pregnancy. If this happens to your bitch, make a make-believe whelping place for her, and provide her with some new toys to substitute for babies.

Select the stud dog in advance—and with care! (Photograph by Billie Jean Shuler)

If your bitch is pregnant, within about two weeks she may be off of her feed for a few days, kind of like morning sickness. Her nipples will be slightly enlarged and quite pink. These may be the only signs you will see until about four to five weeks after the breeding. At that point, you may see a slight rounding out of the abdomen behind the ribs—or, if you are looking down on your bitch, her back may appear broader. If the litter is large, she will bulge more in the middle.

Diet and Exercise

During the pregnancy, your bitch should have an enriched diet and less-than-vigorous exercise. She shouldn't become a couch potato, but running with other dogs and heavy exercise or jumping should be limited, especially in her last month. Consult other breeders for advice on feeding your bitch, and be sure to start her immediately after the breeding on vitamin and mineral supplements.

When she is about six weeks into her pregnancy, the puppies will be growing fast, so you will need to increase your bitch's food amounts accordingly. Give her what she will eat—and most Min Pins will eat whatever you offer. Just be sure it is a proper diet for a pregnant bitch of Min Pin size.

GETTING READY FOR THE BIG EVENT

Prepare the place where the bitch is to whelp at least two weeks ahead of her due date. Whelping boxes of all sizes are available for sale; go to your local pet-supply store and look these boxes over if you want to build one. Again, your breeder can advise you. It's a good idea to have a box that has a ledge around the inside about 4 to 5 inches from the bottom. This will help prevent the bitch from lying down on or sitting on any of her pups.

If you do not have a manufactured whelping box, there are many alternatives. To use a plastic crate, remove the top half of the crate for an instant whelping box that is easy to clean and just the right size for a Miniature Pinscher litter.

The whelping box should be lined with unprinted newspaper, which is available as roll ends from your local newspaper for a small price. If you don't have luck with your local paper, you can also try moving companies, which use this paper to wrap delicate items. At your pet-supply store or at a dog show, purchase several pads of sheepskin or fleece. Use these pads to line the whelping box, and later to line the puppy beds. The pads will absorb fluids and can be easily cleaned in the washer and dryer—you will have to wash and dry them on a daily, if not hourly, basis, depending on how many puppies you have and how fussy you are. You should be *very* fussy.

One popular, inexpensive and efficient whelping box alternative is the bottom half of a plastic crate. (Photograph by Westover)

Be sure that the location of the whelping box is quiet and away from other animals. It should be in a warm, dry place where your bitch will feel secure and unthreatened by activity. Give her plenty of rest time, but let her indicate to you what is best for her.

As your bitch gets closer to her whelping date, she will begin to "nest" in the whelping box. She will dig at the papers and pads, and work at getting them arranged just so. When she goes into labor, her nesting activity is likely to increase. This is a way for her to help with the whelping process as the pups move down through the uterus toward the birth canal. A fairly sure sign that whelping is about to begin is the bitch's temperature, which will drop from its normal range of 101.5°F to 102.5°F, to somewhere around 98°F. She may also refuse a regular meal or any treats, but that is not a reliable sign, especially with a Min Pin.

GESTATION AND WHELPING

The usual gestation period for dogs is 63 days, but this varies also. Count on 60 to 65 days from the date of the *first* successful breeding. With a Min Pin, it is likely that the bitch will whelp earlier than 63 days after conception. If she whelps much before that time, be sure to have your veterinarian give the puppies a thorough examination when he cuts their tails and removes their dewclaws (at 3 or 4 days of age).

If you have not seen a whelping or assisted in one yourself, try to arrange to have an experienced person on call for the time when your bitch goes into labor. If worse comes to worse and you are really nervous about it, just close the door and leave her to nature until help arrives. Assisting in the birth of puppies is a very fine acquired skill; there is a need for swift intervention at times, but most of the work between the bitch and you is similar to a well-orchestrated ballet. You each have a role, and cooperation is vital. Until you've done it, though, you won't know what to do. Read some books with illustrated reports of whelping, and observe another Min Pin whelping, if that is possible.

Min Pins can have as many as six puppies, which makes for a bit of overcrowding. (Photograph by Denetre)

You will need to have on hand for the whelping blunt nosed scissors, cotton thread, a clock and lots of cotton cloths—old washcloths are about the right thing. Old terry kitchen towels work, too. These items are good to rub the puppies in order to get them shouting with deep breaths into their lungs. It also helps in drying them off before you give them back to the bitch. During the whelping, you may want to put each puppy onto a nipple, and they will usually grasp one quite well. When another puppy starts to arrive, put those already born either in a corner of the box, in a separate warm place or up at the front of the bitch, where they will be warm and dry.

When your bitch goes into hard labor (you will see the pinching up of her belly into mounds), start timing. If she is in hard labor for more than one hour without producing a puppy, there may be a problem, and you should contact your veterinarian. This is true of subsequent puppies as well—even when you think the whelping is over, a bitch can fool you and still have one or more pups to deliver. Just be alert to her behavior—that is the best guideline.

Be sure that the sac is broken quickly and that mucus is pressed out of each puppy's nose and mouth. If your bitch is efficient, she will bite the umbilical cord and lick the puppy dry, at the same time stimulating the pup to breathe. If your bitch is reluctant—although Min Pin mothers are exceptionally good—you might have to play nursemaid. In this case, you would cut the cord with your scissors. The cord material stretches, so be sure to make your cut what looks like at least 3 inches from the puppy's belly, pinching the cord between where you will cut and the puppy's belly.

Be absolutely sure that an afterbirth is delivered for each puppy (this is an ugly greenish/black glob of matter that is attached to the other end of the umbilical cord). Some bitches will want to eat the afterbirth, and it is fine to let her do this. Although it is seldom necessary, if excess blood flows from the pup's umbilical cord, tie it off with some of the cotton thread. The more important thing is to get the pup breathing. If you have to play mom, rub the puppy's body vigorously with toweling until you get a good protest from it. Keep rubbing until the puppy squirms, and then get it onto a nipple as soon as possible.

As each puppy is delivered, write down the time of delivery, color, sex and any special comments. This will come in handy later when you are trying to remember just how things went. Once you get the puppies born and get them all onto a nipple for nursing, you can do a bit more for your bitch. Most bitches will welcome a warm mixture of beef bouillon with some canned milk in it. This will replace some of the salts she has lost through the whelping process. She might also welcome some canned meat—beef, heart or kidney canned for dogs or ground fresh will taste good to her. Your bitch will need to be on a good lactation diet

Min Pins are good moms. Once they settle in with their pups, they are contented and the pups will thrive. (Photograph by Captured Critters)

the entire time she is nursing her puppies.

RAISING PUPPIES

When your puppies are 3 or 4 days old, it is customary to have their tails cut. This is not required, but it will probably make it easier to sell your puppies because the Min Pin is normally seen with a short tail and that is probably what your puppy buyer will look for. Be sure to make an appointment with your veterinarian as soon as the puppies are born so that he will be prepared to do the tails on the proper day. Do not let the mother see you take the puppies, and keep her in a room where she cannot go to the whelping box and see that the puppies are gone. She might get totally frantic and feel threatened about the safety of her puppies. On rare occasion, bitches will kill their puppies if they feel overly threatened.

Take a small cardboard box; line it with several layers of toweling or sheepskin fleece, and put the puppies into the box. Cover them with a lightweight towel, and take them to the veterinarian in this way. At the office, do not put the box on any surface except a sterile operating or work table. After the tails and dewclaws have all been done, get the puppies home as soon as possible, and put them back into the whelping box. *Take the smaller transportation box away!* Do not let the bitch see it or smell it. Put the towels into the laundry, and then bring the bitch back into the whelping area to her babies. She will settle down pretty fast.

If all the puppies are eating well and your bitch has sufficient milk, things will be normal. At times, however, you might have to bottle-feed your puppies to supplement their diet. If so, supplements must be given every two hours around the clock, and you will lose a lot of sleep! Some people will not use a bottle but will tube-feed. This can be quite dangerous, and I don't recommend it. If you are told to tube-feed your puppies, get good coaching from your veterinarian or an experienced breeder before you attempt to do this on your own.

Miniature Pinscher puppies generally should have their tails docked at about 4 days of age. (Photograph by Mary Bloom)

Weaning the Puppies

For the first three weeks, the bitch takes care of feeding the puppies and cleaning up after them, and they are pretty happy to stay close to her or in a pile with their littermates. Of course, you'll be doing a lot of laundry, but Mom essentially takes care of the rest.

At about 3 weeks of age, the puppies will have to start the weaning process. This is a gradual process that starts small and finishes at about 6 weeks, with the puppies being completely weaned except for the occasional exposure to their dam who has to be tapered off her milk production. Different breeders have different ways of weaning; consult your breeder friend for a way that is most appropriate for a Min Pin.

Whatever method you use, be sure that the bitch is not in the same room when you are trying to feed the pups. You might let her outside for a little exercise and fresh air. Soon after you start feeding the pups, the bitch will stop cleaning up after them. After all, if you want to be the mom, you have to do the work!

At this time, the accommodations for the pups should be changed from the whelping box. They should be in a puppy pen—it's made for dogs and is like a playpen, but it's made of wire and is raised up off the floor. Some pens have a mesh floor so that excrement falls through to a pan beneath. Put a fleecy bed or snuggle sack at one end of the pen.

The puppies' eyes are open now, and the pups can stagger around. They will crawl away from their bed to relieve themselves. If you give them the opportunity, they will keep themselves clean because they do not like to mess in their own bed. Remember to give them some transition time because the bitch used to clean them up in their bed, and they take a day or so to realize that they have to go somewhere else.

Socialization and Play Time

Although not all experts agree, most students of canine development believe that it is important to handle puppies every day from the moment they are born. In fact, they should be talked to as well, to help them develop proper personalities and self-confidence. If you have chosen names for them, use their names from the very first week onward. Do not call them all "puppy" because they will not grow up with a sense of individuality.

It is best not to let outsiders handle the pups until after they have had their first vaccinations. This is a protective measure, as you never know whether strangers have handled sick dogs and might pass along infectious diseases to your babies. After that, friends who have healthy dogs of their own can handle the pups.

Usually, when the puppies are 3 weeks old, they should be brought out of the whelping area and into the main part of the house, whether the kitchen, the family room or some other area where there is a lot of normal household noise and activity.

Min Pins need lots of petting and handling, and when they are exposed to strangers, they need to be allowed to take the initiative—let them approach strangers. A new place, new sounds and new people should always be introduced with supervision. They'll need a lot of reassurance as they venture into the world, so when you bring them out with you, be aware of their responses.

If no problems arise, the first three weeks of having puppies is a relative breeze. (Photograph by Ellen Michel)

Something as innocuous as a shopping cart can sound and look like a Sherman tank to a dog the size of a Min Pin puppy. As mentioned earlier in the book, you don't want to reinforce a pup's fear by coddling; just be sure that your young dog knows that you're there for him.

Min Pins do need to be introduced to children, but it cannot be overemphasized that these introductions must be done under very careful supervision and circumstances. The child must be instructed on how to approach or hold the puppy, and the child must be sitting down at a low elevation—not in a regular chair—because the puppy is all too likely to leap out of the child's arms and into open space.

No matter how good a puppy's heredity may be, his temperament can be ruined by the lack of early encouragement. In addition to your own

After the pups have had their second series of shots, they can and should be taken everywhere possible out in the world.

activities, enroll your pups in puppy class, where they'll meet other young dogs. These classes are like a kindergarten and can prove very beneficial.

Discerning Show-Quality Puppies

Decisions about show quality are made on the basis of gait, stature, attitude, growth, how the teeth are coming in and whether testicles seem to be developing correctly. Breeder Gloria Knapp shares the Chateau Acres Min Pin growth chart.

Ear Cropping

Min Pins do not need to have their ears cropped if they are going to be companion dogs and not show dogs. If a pup is thought to be of show quality, it is designated for ear cropping by most breeders. Only a licensed veterinarian can properly crop ears, and the procedure is performed while the dog is under anesthesia. Finding a vet that is a true artist with regards to ears can be difficult. Ask your bitch's breeder for input. After the surgery, a great deal of care is needed to prevent infection and to support the shape and carriage of the ear. In some cases, pups are put through more than one surgery with aftercare. A bad taping job can ruin an otherwise beautiful crop, so it is best to let the veterinarian do the taping.

A show dog does not absolutely need to have its ears cropped, although most breeders believe that upright natural ears do not win as often as cropped ears in the show ring. Puppies have drop ears that may or may not become erect as they grow up. Ears that do not come erect are often cropped to give an erect appearance.

SELLING YOUR PUPPIES

First-time breeders usually have no reputation to lean on and so do not have referrals to help them find buyers for their puppies. The neighbors who said they wanted one of Rosie's pups might have decided that a Collie would be better. So what will you do if you have to take care of your puppies until 4 or 6 months of age—or more? Suppose they never sell?

The answer to these and other questions lies in what experienced and responsible breeders do. They don't even consider breeding unless they have cash deposits in advance for their litters. If you are working closely with the breeder from whom you got your bitch, that breeder will probably help you with referrals for your puppies. But there is more to it than just having referrals.

Let's play!

★★★
CHATEAU ACRES MINIATURE PINSCHER GROWTH CHART
★★★

SIZE AT MATURITY	10"	11"	11 1/2"	12"	12 1/2"
AT 8 WEEKS	5 1/2" - 6 1/4"	6 1/4" - 6 1/2"	6 1/2" - 7 1/4"	7 1/4" - 7 3/4"	7 3/4 "- 8"
AT 10 WEEKS	6 1/2" - 6 3/4"	7 " - 8"	8 1/4" - 8 3/4"	8 3/4" - 9 1/4"	9 1/2" - 9 3/4"
AT 12 WEEKS	7 " - 7 1/4"	8" - 8 1/2"	8 3/4" - 9"	9" - 9 1/4"	9 1/2" - 9 3/4"
AT 14 WEEKS	8" - 8 1/4"	9" - 9 1/4"	9 1/4" - 9 3/4"	9 3/4" - 10 1/4"	10 1/4" - 10 1/2"
AT 16 WEEKS	8 1/2" - 9"	9 1/2" - 9 3/4"	9 3/4" - 10 1/4"	10 1/4" - 10 1/2"	10 1/2" - 10 3/4"
AT 18 WEEKS	9" - 9 1/4"	9 3/4 - 10"	10" - 10 1/2"	10 1/2" - 10 3/4"	10 3/4" - 11
AT 20 WEEKS	9 1/4" - 9 1/2"	9 3/4" - 10 1/4"	10 1/4" - 11"	10 1/2" - 11 1/4"	11 1/4" - 11 1/2"
AT 22 WEEKS	9 1/2" - 10"	10 1/4" - 10 3/4"	10 3/4" - 11 1/4"	11 1/4" - 11 3/4"	11 3/4" - 12"
AT 24 WEEKS	10" - 10 1/4"	10 1/2" - 11"	10 7/8" - 11 3/8"	11 1/2" - 12"	11 3/4" - 12 1/4"

A Min Pin Growth Chart. The puppy should show itself off with an outgoing, "choose me" attitude and should stand upright and strong on his four legs that are in perfectly correct position. Final decisions about show or pet quality are often usually made until a puppy is about 6 months of age.

If the ears are uncropped, they might be upright or might have the look of a terrier, which is called a "drop ear."

Registering Your Litter

As soon as your puppies are firmly established in life—when they're 2 or 3 weeks old—you should register your litter with the American Kennel Club.

The Litter Registration Application form is available from the AKC (see Appendix A, "Organizations and More Information"). The owner of the sire of the litter should complete Section A as soon as a successful mating has taken place and the stud service fee has been paid. Be sure to read all of the form, and carefully follow the instructions for completing it. After you submit the completed form and the appropriate fee, the AKC will send you a "litter kit" with a registration application form for each puppy (see Chapter 4, "Finding Your Miniature Pinscher—Puppy, Adult or Rescue," for more information on registering a dog).

Sales Contracts

Sales contracts have become quite common in recent years. As a breeder, you can guarantee only a few qualities of a puppy. You can guarantee the health of your puppy. You can guarantee its heritage with a pedigree. You can guarantee its ability to be registered by means of an application for registration from a registered litter. You can guarantee to buy the puppy back if it does not make a good adjustment in its new home.

No matter how carefully you screen and select your puppy buyers, the one thing you cannot guarantee is what happens to the puppy after it leaves your care. In any case, you must provide some form of contract of sale, which is the buyer's proof of ownership. Your puppies should be identified with a tattoo or a microchip. This is proof to the buyer that the puppy he takes home is the one you have identified as his.

Breeders sometimes try to control what happens to their pups in various ways. The majority of these attempts are worthy because the breeders have the best interests of the puppy in mind. However, some sales requirements are reasonable, and some are not.

Co-ownership

Some breeders feel a need to be in control of everything that happens to their puppies and will sell them only with co-ownership, meaning that the owner cannot breed the dog without the signature of the co-owner. Because people fail to get a tightly written contract for the terms of any co-ownership, this is the significant source of controversy and litigation in the sport.

Co-ownership should be avoided. A better approach is to screen your buyers very carefully and to choose owners you believe you can trust with your puppy.

Conditions of Sale

Some breeders try to maintain control of their puppies by insisting on contracts with all sorts of provisions for future returns, such as getting puppies back from the buyer from litters they might breed or getting puppies back from a breeder as payment for stud services. This is what is commonly called putting strings on a sales agreement. Strings are usually attached to a puppy that is sold at a reduced price. As with co-ownership, putting on or agreeing to strings on a sales contract should be avoided. As a buyer, you wouldn't want to purchase a puppy that came with all sorts of commitments.

Another condition of sale that arises frequently and that can be a decided strain on the buyer is the insistence by the breeder that a puppy be shown to its Championship. There may also be a stipulation that the dog be shown by the breeder or some other professional handler. Even if there is

As a breeder, you want to be sure that your puppies go to owners who care about them just as much as you do. (Photograph by Mary Silfies)

a written contract to this effect, it may not be enforceable because puppies change; ears fail, teeth go bad and accidents can cripple. Then how would this requirement be fulfilled? For your puppy buyers, it is far more reasonable to simply be cooperative and helpful and to offer a lot of encouragement. If things go awry with the puppy, be understanding and empathetic because the buyer will be as disappointed as you are.

Use of Kennel Name

Many breeders use a kennel name in registering their puppies. This is a way of identifying the breeding behind their dogs and is also a form of advertising for the breeder. Once a name is registered, it cannot be changed. Therefore, every time you show or breed your dog or bitch, that breeder's kennel name is carried forward and is before the public—hence, advertising.

If you believe that you are going to be breeding and involved in Min Pins for many, many years, you might want to select or make up a kennel name of your own. This is quite an acceptable practice, and most buyers will go along with your request to use that name in registering their puppies.

Limited Registration

With a limited registration, the dog is registered, but no litters produced by that dog are eligible for registration. The dog that is under limited registration cannot be shown in competitions for Championship points, but it may be exhibited in obedience trials and other licensed events.

Because limited registration status is determined by the litter owner, it is one way to be certain that dogs or bitches that are not of show or breeding quality cannot contribute their faults to the Min Pin registry. Even if they are bred, their puppies cannot be registered. The breeder will obtain a limited registration certificate from the AKC. This certificate is white with an orange border rather than the purple border of a full registration certificate. On rare occasion, the limited registration can be changed, but only at the request of the breeder of the litter. If you plan to sell a puppy with a limited registration, be certain that the buyer understands all the implications and agrees to the limitation. A signed acknowledgment is suggested.

Spaying and Neutering

All dogs that are sold as pets should be spayed or neutered. Terms covering spaying or neutering are common in Min Pin sales contracts. For one thing, there is evidence that spayed or neutered animals live a longer, healthier life. Although males can be neutered prior to their hormonal maturity, spaying must wait until the bitch is mature. In Min Pins, this will be about 18 months of age. By this age, a

Many breeders require owners of pet Min Pins to spay or neuter their dog. This policy helps prevent an overabundance of dogs and helps maintain the best qualities in the breed. (Photograph by Mary Bloom)

bitch will have reached her full physical and mental maturation.

Spaying and neutering also is a responsible way of controlling the unwanted pet population and is part of your responsibility as a reputable Min Pin breeder. Having puppies for the sake of having puppies or "so that the children can learn the facts of life" is not at all wise. Only the best dogs should be reserved for breeding purposes.

Retired show dogs and retired brood bitches are often spayed or neutered when they are no longer to be used for breeding. Indeed, long-time breeders support spaying and neutering of their retired dogs. Most breeders will take care of the neutering process before placing their retired Min Pins in homes as pets.

If your prospective pet puppy buyer will not agree to spay or neuter, sell the puppy on a limited registration, or don't sell to that person.

The Puppy Pack

Each puppy should be accompanied by a "puppy pack" on its departure from your home. This should include information on health care and health requirements the new owner must fulfill (shots and worming, for example). Include a supply of the food and vitamins the puppy is accustomed to having. If the buyer does not have a veterinarian, you should supply recommendations to veterinarians in the area. Information and educational pamphlets also are available from the Miniature Pinscher Club of America and the American Kennel Club, and you should include these in the puppy pack.

Of course, your puppy pack will include a copy of the puppy's pedigree and the appropriate registration form. You also might want to include one of the toys the litter has played with, as a reassurance to the pup; a new toy is in order as well.

Any other items of comfort are optional, such as a new sheepskin or fleece.

Counsel the buyer about the puppy's crate and other equipment needs. Before the new owner picks up the pup, remind him of those items that he should have waiting for the pup at home.

Follow-Up Support

After the puppies have left your home, it is a good idea to provide some supportive, friendly follow-up. Call the new owners after a few days. Be sure they have taken the pup to their veterinarian for a checkup and that all is well. Be sure they are bonding with the pup and that feeding is going well. Most importantly, emphasize that you are available for help and advice, and *reemphasize* that if anything does not go well, you will take the puppy back to train it or to replace it. Your responsibilities as a breeder never end.

(Photograph by Warfield)

CHAPTER THIRTEEN

Special Care
for the Older Dog

"If you don't want to have a dog for 12 to 17 years, don't get a Min Pin."
—NORMA CACKA, BREEDER

Older Min Pins, like any breed, rate special consideration. As they grow older, these dogs are like aging humans. They might have specific ailments, or their physical machinery might begin to wear out or need replacement parts. The person acquiring a young Min Pin must realize that the dog will most likely live into old age, so owners must be aware of the needs of a geriatric dog.

Once the Min Pin decides he is a show dog, that attitude never leaves him. As the dogs age, they sometimes can be shown in veteran classes (usually specified for dogs and bitches over 7 years of age). Min Pins still are fierce competitors into their sunset years.

Special care for the older dog is similar to the care you might give yourself. A few specifics need attention.

This dog, once a true red, now has a clearly graying coat. Notice that she retains all her other wonderful Min Pin characteristics. (Photograph by Tucker)

WEIGHT WATCHING

In our health-conscious society, we are more aware of the dangers of obesity. And we also know how much more difficult it becomes to keep weight off and maintain fitness as we age. Obesity is just as bad for your dog and just as difficult to control.

What Causes Obesity?

Obesity is caused by one or more of the following:

- Improper diet
- Too little exercise
- Systemic disorders

The next sections address these problems in more detail.

Improper Diet

Just like humans, a Min Pin is much more active when he is younger. At that time, he is "growing into his skin" and is fed a richer diet with more of the nutrients his growing body needs. It is at this time also that bad habits get established, such as feeding treats from the table or other treats all day long. Dogs can only assimilate what they actually need, so the rest is over the limit. Min Pins tend to be food vacuum cleaners anyway, so owners must exercise restraint and take care not to overfeed.

Specific foods on the market can help prevent or adjust obesity, just as there are special foods available for various ills. Your veterinarian can advise you about your aging dog's diet.

Too Little Exercise

When your Min Pin is younger, he will exercise more than your aging dog. As you notice your dog naturally wanting to lead a less active life, his food intake will have to be cut back in proportion.

Along with too little exercise comes slower circulation and more chills. Your pensioner will appreciate a warm sweater and a wool blanket.

Systemic Disorders

Some problems with endocrine functions or digestive processes might cause your dog to gain weight no matter what you do to prevent it. Often, these types of problems make it difficult for the dog to even go for its regular walks. More often, there is a problem with the way the dog assimilates what limited food you give him. Again, your

Min Pins are always active, but the aging dog will seem to take more naps and not be quite as active as you have come to expect. When you are certain that he is not ill, just think of your older dog as being 70 or 80 and deserving of a rest now and then.

veterinarian will be the most important source of diagnosis and advice.

Managing Obesity

Simply put, treat your older dog with consideration and understanding. In the same way you go for your annual checkups, he needs to see his veterinarian on a regular basis. If any signs of illness occur, they obviously call for a visit to your dog's favorite veterinarian. Prevention is the most important way to keep your Min Pin trim and

Even pups enjoy a sweater in cold weather. This youngster may be wearing his grandpa's favorite. (Photograph by Warfield)

healthy. Problems that are caught early can be resolved more readily. Older Min Pins tend to be set in their ways as well, so their regular routines should be maintained as much as possible.

VISION AND HEARING

These problems of human aging do not bypass the older dog, either. In fact, failing eyesight and loss of hearing are common in dogs over 8 to 10 years of age.

Vision

In their later years, Min Pins may lose their sight from cataracts. You will probably notice a cloudiness in one or both eyes that will call for a visit to the veterinarian. Cataracts can be removed if treated early.

Hearing

Another concern in aging Min Pins is hearing loss. This is very difficult for a Min Pin to accept. Remember that your dog's hearing is acute and that it helps him be the great watchdog that he is. When his ability to hear diminishes, the dog may feel disoriented and appear withdrawn or depressed. If your dog has lost his hearing, young dogs and children are likely to startle and annoy him, just as they might if the dog's

Be thoughtful of your aging dog's abilities. If his hearing diminishes, don't be annoyed with him when he doesn't answer your call right away. (Photograph by Mary Bloom)

eyesight is poor. Try to protect him from these disturbances.

MAINTAINING A SENIOR'S HEALTH

Infected or loose teeth, rheumatism, arthritis and other aches and pains are all potential problems in the older Min Pin. Some health issues can be prevented with a regular routine of care from a young age. Other difficulties are just a matter of aging.

These are not avoidable altogether, but you can take steps to keep your senior dog comfortable and happy.

As your dog ages, be careful to keep him away from drafts because he is likely to be more susceptible to the cold. Although he'll still need some exercise, he should be kept relatively quiet. Make sure that your Min Pin is kept clean. Because his kidneys may not be as strong as they once were, he may need more frequent hygiene breaks. You certainly don't want him to be uncomfortable, so let him out a little more often. The aging dog is more dependent on you than ever and will appreciate your care and consideration.

WHEN THE END IS NEAR

There comes a time when we must face the fact that our senior friends cannot stay with us forever. Maybe your dog is just old. Certainly, if he is in pain, you should have no question in your mind about relieving him of that suffering. Your dog trusts you and relies on you to do the best thing for him. Your dog has loved you with never-wavering devotion, and he knows in his heart that you will help him when the time comes. It is never easy, but the dog will tell you in his eyes when it's the right time.

Your veterinarian will once again guide you during this difficult time and can help you determine whether your dog should be euthanized. Some owners like to be present when the dog is given his injection; it is a way to be with the dog and reassure him right up to the end. It also is comforting to be there while he goes peacefully to sleep with your voice speaking to him and your hand holding and stroking him.

Your veterinarian can advise you about cremation possibilities. In many areas, your dog can be interred in a lovely and appealing pet cemetery with an appropriate stone or marker. There is always the option of burial on your own property, if that is a place where you plan to live for a long time. (Sometimes it's hard to leave these friends behind.) Another choice that many people make is to have their dog cremated and then keep the urn somewhere in the house. No matter what choice you make, when it is done at the right time, it will be the right choice.

Grieving

It's important to recognize that you will feel a deep-seated grief for the loss of your dear dog. Some people rush right out and get another dog to "replace" the lost one. Of course, that is not possible—there is no way to replace that dog. You might build a close relationship with another new dog, but it takes time. Even if you have lots of dogs and friends say, "How lucky you are—you have lots of dogs, so it won't be so hard for you," they couldn't be more wrong. There is no way to even pretend that all the dogs are the same. Your relationship with each of your dogs is special; there will never be another one just like the one you lost.

At some time, you will relate in a different way but just as closely with another dog, but that dog

Your Min Pin is special to you in his unique way. Don't be ashamed to grieve the loss of your dog. (Photograph by Candids by Connie)

might be entirely different. Think how unfair it would be to expect another dog to fill those vacant shoes of your one and only great Min Pin. When you are ready, you must accept any new dogs at face value and learn to know them as they are without any attempt to make them like the dog you loved and lost.

Sometimes your family or your friends may not understand your grief. "How can you be so upset about a *dog*?" they might ask. They don't understand that your Min Pin wasn't just a dog—he was your best friend and confidante. He would have understood how you feel and would not have questioned your feelings at all.

Am I Going Crazy?

You hear his paw steps. You feel for him with your foot at the bottom of the bed. You hear him sneeze! You find yourself fixing his favorite special dinner. You cry. You talk to him. You don't want any other dogs near you. You are depressed. No, you are not going crazy. All these occurrences are natural. Many people will not understand and will be insulted by the idea, but you will go through the five phases of grieving just as you would if you had lost a beloved human best friend.

1. At first, you will be in shock and denial. You will tell everyone, "I'm okay—I have another dog at home," or "I'm getting another dog tomorrow." You will tell yourself that it was the best thing to do and that it is really crazy to grieve over a dog. You will work very hard to not allow yourself to feel what you are feeling.

2. Then there is a kind of "poor me" phase. You'll feel sorry for yourself, with questions like, "Why did *my* dog have to die?" and "Why didn't he live longer?" and "Why didn't the vet find the problem sooner?"

3. Then you will get angry. You will be angry that your dog died, that your family doesn't understand and that dogs are around at all. You will be snappish with everyone, including any other dogs you might have. But they will understand.

4. Then there is a kind of bargaining phase. You might tell yourself, "I'll never get another dog," or, "I'll get another dog today," or, "I'll go home and be so kind to all my other pets that I won't miss my dog at all." It won't work.

5. Finally, there will be acceptance. You will have cried yourself out. You will have snapped at everyone around you. You will have rejected efforts of your other dog or dogs to make you feel better. And you will have finally come to a point where you begin to have happy memories of the dog you lost. You will see how cute your other dog is. You will make an effort to get into a deeper relationship with another dog in the house, or you will be ready to go and begin to look for another puppy.

Easing the Pain

Yes, it will hurt, but there are ways to ease your pain. If you are really feeling grief that you can't seem to control, see a counselor. This will be someone you can cry with and talk to. It feels good to have a comforting professional who is understanding and who doesn't judge your attachment to your dog.

Many people find comfort in making a special scrapbook of and about their dog. Shop for an attractive scrapbook and other supplies that will express the unique qualities of your Min Pin. If you make a real project out of it, this will help you see the wonderful memories you have of your dog and obtain a sense of closure that his special little life is over.

You Are Not Alone

If you have more than one Min Pin, as many people do, take care to understand the grieving of the dog or dogs left behind. A Min Pin can attach himself so closely to another dog or to one of his humans that he runs the danger of grieving unto death after the death of his loved one. It is possible that you and another grieving dog can bond through this grief and support and comfort each other.

Signs of grieving in your dog might include withdrawal, excess sleeping, lack of interest in food or normal activities, irritability and a noticeable change in personality. If these symptoms persist for more than a week or ten days, consult your veterinarian for help.

(Photograph by Warfield)

CHAPTER FOURTEEN

The Miniature Pinscher Club of America

". . . To preserve and protect the Miniature Pinscher . . ."
—MINIATURE PINSCHER CLUB OF AMERICA

THE CLUB AND ITS OBJECTIVES

Yes, the Miniature Pinscher Club of America does exist! The organization was formed and recognized by the American Kennel Club in 1929, and several localized Min Pin clubs are spread throughout the United States. You can contact a coordinator for local clubs for information on a club in your area.

The MPCA, referred to as the Parent Club, holds an annual Specialty Show between March 1 and June 30 each year, with a rotating location. The specialty show is a multiple-day event with educational seminars, puppy sweepstakes, conformation and obedience competitions and agility contests. This is the only place where you might see more than 300 Min Pins all in one location.

Each member of the MPCA receives the official publication, called "Pinscher Patter," which is mailed quarterly and contains a wealth of information on the breed. Articles pertain to the Min Pin—and sometimes dogs in general—and the newsletter also features pictures of recent winners.

CLUB COMMITTEES

The MPCA has many committees designed to cover all aspects of owning, showing, breeding and loving a Min Pin. These committees include the following:

AKC Gazette Reporter
Awards and Plaques
Breeders' Directory
Futurity
Health and Welfare of the Min Pin
Historian
Judges' Education
Legislation
Local Clubs
Members' Education
Membership
National Breed Club Alliance
Nominations
Obedience Awards
"Pinscher Patter"
Public Education
Rescue Coordinator
Specialty Guidelines
Top Ten Min Pins
Webmaster

   As you can see, no stone is left unturned.

The MPCA can provide you with lots of information on how to care for your Miniature Pinscher. (Photograph by Mary Bloom)

CURRENT INFORMATION AND CONTACTS

Through the wonders of modern technology, you can find the name and address of just about anyone connected with the MPCA on the organization's Web page at http://members.aol.com/mpcapec/mpcafaqs.html.

This address will get you through to one of the most colorful and beautifully designed Web pages on the Net. You can find all current information there, including pictures of recent National Specialty winners, illustrations of the different coat colors, types of ears on Min Pins and the latest news on what's happening in the world of Min Pins.

If you are not computer-friendly, contact the American Kennel Club or the Miniature Pinscher Club of America (see Appendix A, "Organizations and More Information") for other contacts.

(Photograph by Warfield)

Organizations and More Information

American Kennel Club
260 Madison Ave.
New York, NY 10016

OR

American Kennel Club
5580 Centerview Dr., Suite 200
Raleigh, NC 27606-3390
900-407-PUPS (7877)
www.akc.org/akc/
e-mail: info@akc.org

Canine Eye Research Foundation (CERF)
Veterinary Medical Data Program
South Campus Courts, Building C
Purdue University
West Lafayette, IN 47907

Internet Miniature Pinscher Service (IMPS)
Independent Internet Min Pin Rescue Services
877-646-7461
http://members.xoom.com/minpinrescue
e-mail: harkon@inexpress.net

Miniature Pinscher Club of America
Attn: Ms. Trudy Roundy, Secretary
1196 Teakwood Dr.
Taylorsville, UT 84123
e-mail: shadara@aros.net

Miniature Pinscher Club of America
Breeder's Referral Service
Attn: Ms. Betty Cottle
332 MacArthur Circle
Cocoa, FL 32927

Miniature Pinscher Club of America
National Rescue Coordinator
Attn: Susan Goldman
6906 Woodbridge Dr.
Norfolk, VA 23518
e-mail: altanero@picusnet.com

Miniature Pinscher Club of America Web Page
http://members.aol.com/mpcapec/mpcafaqs.html

National Association for Search and Rescue
P.O. Box 3709
Fairfax, VA 22309

National Dog Registry
Lost and Found
P.O. Box 116
Woodstock, NY 12498

Orthopedic Foundation for Animals (OFA)
University of Missouri
Columbia, MO 65211

Therapy Dogs International
6 Hilltop Rd.
Mendham, NJ 07945

United Kennel Club
100 E. Kilgore Rd.
Kalamazoo, MI 49001

U.S. Dog Agility Association
P.O. Box 850955
Richardson, TX 75085

The Miniature Pinscher Club of America Code of Ethics

The Miniature Pinscher Club of America is dedicated to furthering the health and soundness of the breed.

CODE OF ETHICS

This code is established in accordance with the objectives of the Miniature Pinscher Club of America, Inc. (MPCA). It is presented for the use of MPCA members when buying, breeding, selling and exhibiting Miniature Pinschers. Violations of the MPCA Code of Ethics will be subject to prompt action under MPCA grievance and charge procedures, and may be grounds for expulsion.

(Photograph by Jacobson Studio)

1. Abide by the Constitution and By-Laws of the MPCA and the rules and decisions of the American Kennel Club (AKC).

2. Maintain accurate breeding records, registrations and pedigrees, and never knowingly falsify such records. At the time of sale, furnish a pedigree and AKC registration or transfer documents to each buyer unless written agreement is made at time of sale that papers are being withheld.

3. All services and sales arrangements shall be mutually agreed upon and should be stated in writing, signed by all parties involved, including all adjustments, replacement conditions, etc.

4. Maintain the best possible standards of canine health, cleanliness, and care, and see that puppies are immunized and checked for parasites. Not place puppies under eight weeks of age in a new home. Furnish a complete written health record and care and feeding instructions with each puppy or adult sold.

5. Honestly evaluate the structural and mental qualities of all Miniature Pinschers sold, fairly represent the dogs, and set prices based on individual quality. Maintain prices so as not to be injurious to the breed or other members. Encourage the spaying or neutering of animals not desirable for breeding, and sell them on limited registration, or with written agreement to withhold papers pending the animal being altered.

6. Breed only mature animals in good health, free from communicable diseases and major genetic faults. Stud service will not be offered to bitches not meeting these criteria, or to unregistered bitches. No bitch may be bred for commercial reasons, and no stud dog may be bred to a bitch whose owner is directly or indirectly involved with puppy mills; brokers who purchase litter lots or individuals for re-sale to pet shops or other commercial facilities; pet shops; research laboratories; or commercial enterprises involved in like activities.

7. No Miniature Pinscher may be sold to commercial facilities; research laboratories; pet shops; brokers who purchase litter lots or individuals for re-sale to pet shops or other commercial facilities, puppy mills or their agents. Miniature Pinschers will not be offered for raffles, auctions or as prizes in any "give away" schemes.

8. Encourage and support the MPCA Health and Welfare Committee, with specific attention to testing for health disorders directly relating to Miniature Pinschers.

9. All advertising shall be honest, as factual as possible, and not misrepresentative, exaggerated, fraudulent or misleading. Deceptive or untrue statements about the dogs or practices of others will not be made.

10. Conduct all affairs in a fair, honest and ethical manner. Act, at all times in a manner which reflects favorably on the Club, its membership, the sport of purebred dog showing and Miniature Pinschers in particular. This includes respect for show sites, hotels and all other aspects of dog ownership.

(Photograph by Mary Bloom)

Titles Available to the Miniature Pinscher

CONFORMATION

Champion	Ch.

OBEDIENCE

Companion Dog	CD
Companion Dog Excellent	CDX
Utility Dog	UD
Utility Dog Excellent	UDX
Tracking Dog	TD
Tracking Dog Excellent	TDX
Variable Surface Tracking	VST
Obedience Trial Champion	OTCH
Champion Tracking Dog	CT

AGILITY

Novice Agility Dog	NA
Novice Agility Jumper with Weaves	NAJ
Open Agility Dog	OA
Open Agility Jumper with Weaves	OAJ
Agility Dog Excellent	AX
Excellent Jumper with Weaves	AXJ
Master Agility Excellent	MX
Master Excellent Jumper with Weaves	MXJ
Agility Champion	MACH

Miniature Pinscher Club of America Hall of Fame and Honor Roll

Hall of Fame and Honor Roll statistics presented here are based on the American Kennel Club Awards Publication through December 1998. For further updates, check the MPCA Web site at http://members.aol.com/mpcapec/index.html.

HALL OF FAME SIRES (20 CHAMPIONS TO QUALIFY)

Ch. Carlee Nubby Silk (116)

Ch. Bo-Mar's Road Runner (73)

Ch. Sanbrook Silk Electric (72)

Ch. Shajawn's Free Hand (68)

Ch. Redwings On the Cutting Edge (48)

Ch. Carlee Southern Prancer (47)

Ch. Rebel Roc's Casanova Von Kurt (47)

Ch. Shajawn Semi Tough (45)

Ch. Von Dorf's Dominator (37)

Ch. King Eric V Konigsbach (36)

Ch. Bo-Mar's Drummer Boy (35)
Ch. Sunsprite Eli V Chateau Acres (35)
Ch. Ruffians Starbuck (30)
Ch. Delcrest Gold Nugget (29)
Ch. Shieldcrest Cinnamon Toast (29)
Ch. Halrok Headliner (28)
Ch. Rebel Roc's Jackpot (28)
Ch. Sanbrook Impossible Scheme (28)
Ch. Jay-Mac's Moon Eagle (27)
Ch. Fillpin's Madric Lucas (26)
Ch. Sunsprite Luth'r Of Pevensey (24)
Bel-Roc's Snicklefritz V Enztal (23)
Ch. Elan's Shiloh V Whitehouse (23)
Ch. Jay-Mac's Pippin (23)
Ch. Parker's Guardian Angel (23)
Ch. Sanbrook Smooth Operator (22)
Ch. Sanbrook Masked Warrior (22)
Ch. Sunsprite Night Games (22)
Ch. Ariston's Knight Rider (21)
Ch. Bluehen's Solidgoldgntleman (21)
Ch. Jay-Mac's Pat Hand (21)
Ch. King Allah V Siegenburg (20)
Ch. Mercer's Desert Dust Devil (20)
Ch. Pevensey Gold Prospector (20)
Reh-Mont's Artistry In Rhythm (20)
Ch. Sunsprite Silk Dandy (20)
Ch. Whitnel Thunderhead (20)

HALL OF FAME DAMS
(8 CHAMPIONS TO QUALIFY)

Ch. Jay-Mac's Silk Stockings (25)
Ch. Jay-Mac's Ramblin Rose (22)

Ch. Gypsey of Alema (19)
Ch. Redwing's Above Suspicion (19)
Rolling Greens Sparkle (17)
Ch. Carlee Classie Chassie (16)
Ch. Parker's Second Hand Rose (16)
Goldmedal Girl of Shamrock (15)
Ch. Reh-Mont's Dinah Lee (14)
Ch. Rocky Point Penny Ante (13)
Ch. Jay-Mac's Miss Michigan (12)
Sanbrook Silk All Over (12)
Ch. Blythewood Me Jane (11)
Ch. Gaela Run For the Roses (11)
Ch. Granbar's Glamour Girl (11)
Onlyone Perpetual Motion (11)
Bergeron's Miss Heidi (10)
Ch. Blythewood I'll Turn You On (10)
Ch. Marlex Electra Madness (10)
Mile-Bet's Dancing Doll (10)
Ch. Carlee Careless Love (9)
Ch. Carlee Southern Exposure (9)
Ch. Halrok Halla Luya (9)
Ch. Mara's Pinot Chardonnay (9)
Ch. Pevensey's Ciara (9)
Rika's Rolling Pin V Jecamo (9)
Ch. Sanbrook Stage Struck (9)
Ch. Sanbrook Wrapped In Silk (9)
Ch. Shajawn American Dream (9)
Ch. Bluehen's Touch Of Class (8)
Ch. Blythewood I'll Lite Your Fire (8)
Ch. Bud-Lee's Spittin' Image (8)
Ch. Carlee Cover Me In Silk (8)
Ch. Carlee Love Unlimited (8)
Ch. Carlee Satin Sachet (8)
Cox's Miss Dynamite (8)
Ch. Mercer's Desert Storm (8)

Ch. Mercer's Ida Redbird (8)
Ch. Merrywood's Once Upon A Time (8)
Ch. Parker's Ruby Red Dress (8)
Ch. Reh-Mont's Sweet Georgia Brown (8)
Ch. Rollin Roc's Queen Royale (8)
Ch. Sanbrook Fantasy In Silk (8)
Ch. Sanbrook Swept Away (8)
Sanbrook Sultana (8)

HONOR ROLL OF SIRES
(11 CHAMPIONS TO QUALIFY)

Ch. Bandbox Cut The Bull
Ch. Baron Anthony Von Meyer
Ch. Bel-Roc's Yancy V Enztal
Ch. Blythewood Too Hot To Handle
Ch. Bo-Mar's Pepper Pot V Enztal
Ch. Captain Perkio
Carlee Mcshains The Name
Ch. Chateau Acres Freeway Freddy
Ch. Gil-Pin's Southern Gentleman
Ch. Helm's Gunner General
Ch. Jay-Mac's Stepping Stone
Ch. Jay-Mac's Top Hand
Ch. Jay-Mac's Top Roller
Ch. K-Box Lord Dexter of Rigadoon
Ch. King Pin's Hawkeye
Ch. Kloeber's I'm a Superman
Ch. Krane's Sweet Woodruff
Ch. K-Roc's Kopper Kidd
Ch. Madric's Motown Magic
Ch. March on Moremusic Less Talk
Ch. Marykins Jeremy

Ch. Midnight Sun V Haymount
Ch. Pine Hollow's Peter Pan
Ch. Pleasants Go For It
Ch. Reh-Mont's Road Knight
Ch. Rei Mars Chip Off The Ol' Bloc
Ch. Ric-Lor's Running Wild
Ch. Sanbrook Sentry V Spritelee
Ch. Sanbrook Show Down
Ch. Sanbrook Showpiece
Ch. Sanbrook The Sentinel
Ch. Shajawn Free For All
Ch. Star-M Evel Knievel, CDX
Ch. Sunbrook Smooth Character
Ch. Sunnyside's Chico Man
Ch. Sunsprite Bet-R Hi Roller
Tanglewood's Brown Wind Up Toy
Ch. Von Dorf's Free Spirit
Ch. Von Enztal's Black Velvet
Ch. Whitehouse's Te 'n Te
Ch. Whitnel John Boy

HONOR ROLL OF DAMS
(6 CHAMPIONS TO QUALIFY)

Ch. Ariston's Mariko
Ch. Bailess Zinderilla
Ch. Barpin-Sanbrook Sunburst
Ch. Barpin of Coral, CDX
Bel-Roc's Krissie V Enztal
Ch. Bel-Roc's Sugar V Enztal
Bluehen's Roses Are Red
Ch. Blythewood Black Licorice
Ch. Bo-Mar's Ebony Belle

Bo-Mar's Kentucky Lake Mimi

Ch. Brad-Lo's Merrie Melody

Ch. Bronze Trinket Von Milhaus

Ch. Bu-Bic's Kiss Me Kate

Ch. Carron's Doing It In The Buf

Ch. Carron-Lebijou Scarlet Fever

Ch. Carwyn's Beauty Ii

Ch. Cass-Lyne Teri Deb

Chateau Acres Almond Joy

Ch. Chateau Acres Brandy

Ch. Chateau Acres Candy Girl

Ch. Chateau Acres Funny Girl

Ch. Chateau Acres Gun Moll

Dascom Della

Delcrest Paddy Wack

Der Stutz Fawn Memories, CD

Ch. Driftwinds Mighty Foxfire

Ch. Fillpin's Salinda of Jay-Mac

Ch. Halrok Happy Talk

Ch. Halrok Hot Ticket

Ch. Happywalk's Tip Off

Hel-Len's Change For a Penny

Ch. Jay-Mac's Bicentennial Rose

Ch. Jay-Mac's Caroline

Jay-Mac's Love Song

Ch. Kentucky Lakes' Gait-A-Way Mimi

Ch. Kloebers Super Star Bergeron

Krane's Brandi Wine

Ch. Lady Trisha V Milhaus

Madric's Jubilee

Ch. March-On Motivation

Ch. March-On Strike My Hart

Ch. Mcshain Gofor Gold Shajawn

Ch. Mcshain's Lola Of Ruffian

Ch. Milebet Mistress of Metcourt

Mitternacht V D Niemanhoff

Music City Misty Teardrop

Ch. Parker's Penny Serenade

Ch. Pevensey Sara V Chateau Acre

Ch. Pevensey Share the Dream

Ch. Pevenseys Classy Carlee

Ch. Phase-Two Antonia

Ch. Pine Hollow's No Doubt About It

Pine Hollow Rollin Roc Jo Jo

Pros Hot Little Angel

Ch. Rebel Roc's Ballerina Von Kurt

Ch. Redwing Roundelay V Wen-Rose

Ch. Reh-Mont's Brown Skin Gal

Ch. Reh-Mont's I Got Rhythm

Ch. Rrydal's Roses Are Red

Ch. San Antonio's Rebel

Ch. Sanbrook China Silk

Sanbrook Moon Stone

Ch. Sanbrook Sparkling Silk

Ch. Sanbrook Stolenkiss

Sandsturm I'm A Soul Sister

Ch. Sandy Hill Sheba's Flicka

Ch. Shajawn Obra Maestra Mcshain

Sprague's Miss Holiday

Ch. Star-M Temptation

Ch. Sunbrook Indian Amber

Ch. Tammy V Clowalk

Ch. Teddi's K H Carrie

Ch. Top Hat Sweet Scarlet

Ch. Tri-Lem's Entertainer

Ch. Von Frohlich's Schatzie

Westerholz Black Velvet

White House Gabriel

Ch. Wil-B's Marcia V Song

Wil-B's Musical Fantasy V Song

CHAMPION PRODUCING KENNELS

This compilation of statistics of number of Champions over 31 produced by each kennel was reported in "Pinscher Patter," December 1997.

Sanbrook	139
Bo-Mar	115
Jay-Mac	102
Sunsprite	86
Chateau Acres	83
Madric	55
Wil-B's	55
Geddesberg	52
Pevensey	52
OnlyOne	51
March-On	46
Bailes	45
Blythwood	45
Bluehens	44
Delcrest	40
Parker	40
Whitehouse	40
Brad-Lo	39
Carlee	39
Halrok	38
Pros/Provencio	38
Hillview's	37
Rebel Roc	36
Shajawn	35
Kloeber	33
Von Der Fess	33
Goldmedal	32
Rehmont	32

(Photograph by Booth Photography)

Miniature Pinscher Club of America National Specialty Winners

1999   Orlando, Florida

Best of Breed: Ch. Roadshow Steppin On The Edge
High in Trial: Sultans Lovin' Siren, UD

1998   Fort Worth, Texas

Best of Breed: Ch. Whitehouse's Hot Damm—
   Here I Am!
High in Trial: Sultans Lovin' Siren, CDX

1997   Vancouver, Washington

Best of Breed: Ch. Marlex Mercedes
High in Trial: Burgundy Bit of Sugar and Spice,
UD

1996   Holyoke, Massachusetts

Best of Breed: Ch. Lu Lin Jerry Lee
High in Trial: Timline's Hello Ruby Red Doll, CD

1995   Anaheim, California

Best of Breed: Ch. Hackberry Syrus
High in Trial: Sultan's Lovin' Siren, CD

1994   Louisville, Kentucky

Best of Breed: Ch. Chateau Acres Flackey Jake
High in Trial: Fairhaven's Impulsive Mia, UD

1993   Ft. Lauderdale, Florida

Best of Breed: Ch. Redwings on the Cutting Edge
High in Trial: Der Stutz Zelda Zing, UD

1992   Vancouver, Washington

Best of Breed: Ch. Redwings on the Cutting Edge
High in Trial: Mity Tiny Hitter, CDX

1991   Leesburg, Virginia

Best of Breed: Ch. Sanbrook Silk Electric
High in Trial: High Spirit Spider Man

1990   Chicago, Illinois

Best of Breed: Ch. Sunbrook Buckskin Gal
High in Trial: Rocky Road's Wiseguy, CDX

1989   Irving, Texas

Best of Breed: Ch. Sanbrook Silk Electric
High in Trial: Der Stutz Zelda Zing, CD

1988   Spokane, Washington

Best of Breed: Ch. Sanbrook Silk Electric
High in Trial: Mity Tiny Hitter, CD

1987   Springfield, Massachusetts★

Best of Breed: Ch. Pevensey's Cash Dividend

1986   Louisville, Kentucky

Best of Breed: Ch. Pine Hollow's Peter Pan

1986   Anaheim, California

Best of Breed: Ch. Bee Jay's Photo Finish

1985   Vancouver, Washington

Best of Breed: Ch. Mercer's Desert Dust Devil

1985   Irving, Texas

Best of Breed: Ch. Sunsprite Saxon of Carlee

1984   Tampa, Florida

Best of Breed: Ch. Sanbrook Simplicity

1984   Philadelphia, Pennsylvania

Best of Breed: Ch. Sanbrook Sahara

★ *Prior to 1988, no classes for Obedience were offered at the National Specialty.*

1983   Tucson, Arizona
Best of Breed: Ch. Carlee Nubby Silk

1983   Chicago, Illinois
Best of Breed: Ch. Mercer's Desert Dust Devil

1982   Santa Barbara, California
Best of Breed: Ch. Carlee Nubby Silk

1982   Chicago, Illinois
Best of Breed: Ch. Carlee Nubby Silk

1981   Irving, Texas
Best of Breed: Ch. Shajawn Semi Tough

1981   Chicago, Illinois
Best of Breed: Ch. Fillpin's Serendipity

1980   Springfield, Massachusetts
Best of Breed: Ch. Onlyone Chocolate Bon Bon

1980   Chicago, Illinois
Best of Breed: Ch. Mercer's Desert Dust Devil

1979   Dallas, Texas
Best of Breed: Ch. Pine Hollow's Peter Pan

1979   Chicago, Illinois
Best of Breed: Ch. Shinyas Pipe Dream

1978   Pasadena, California
Best of Breed: Ch. Joy's Lady Ginger

1978   Chicago, Illinois
Best of Breed: Ch. Mercer's Desert Dust Devil

1977   Springfield, Massachusetts
Best of Breed: Ch. Mercer's Desert Dust Devil

1977   Chicago, Illinois
Best of Breed: Reh-Mont's I Got Rhythm

1976   Tempe, Arizona
Best of Breed: Mercer's Desert Dust Devil

1976   Chicago, Illinois
Best of Breed: Ch. Jay-Mac's Dream Walking

1975   Dallas, Texas
Best of Breed: Ch. Jay-Mac's Impossible Dream

1975   Chicago, Illinois
Best of Breed: Ch. Top Hat Arabella

1974   Dallas, Texas
Best of Breed: Ch. Jay-Mac's Impossible Dream

1974   Chicago, Illinois
Best of Breed: Ch. Jay-Mac's Pat Hand

1973   Portland, Oregon
Best of Breed: Ch. K-Roc's Black Doubloon

1973   Chicago, Illinois
Best of Breed: Ch. Jay-Mac's Impossible Dream

1972   Dallas, Texas
Best of Breed: Jay-Mac's Candy Man

1972   Chicago, Illinois
Best of Breed: Star-M Trace of Scarlet

1971   Chicago, Illinois
Best of Breed: Ch. Allens Brandy Snifter

1970   Chicago, Illinois
Best of Breed: Ch. Jay-Mac's Jacqueline

1969   Chicago, Illinois
Best of Breed: Ch. Helm's Nero

1968   Chicago, Illinois
Best of Breed: Ch. Rebel Roc's Star Boarder

1967   Chicago, Illinois
Best of Breed: Ch. Rebel Roc's Star Boarder

1966   Chicago, Illinois
Best of Breed: Ch. Rebel Roc's Jackpot

1965   Chicago, Illinois
Best of Breed: Ch. Bo-Mar's Drummer Boy

1964   Chicago, Illinois
Best of Breed: Ch. Shieldcrest Cinnamon Toast

Bibliography and References

BOOKS

American Kennel Club. *The Complete Dog Book,* 19th ed. revised. New York: Howell Book House, 1997.

American Kennel Club. *The Complete Dog Book.* Garden City, New York: Halcyon House, 1943.

Bagshaw, Margaret R. *Pet Miniature Pinscher.* Fond du Lac, Wisconsin: All Pets Books, Inc., 1958.

Bagshaw, Margaret R. *Pet Miniature Pinscher.* Fond du Lac, Wisconsin: All Pets Books, Inc., 1956.

Bauman, Diane. *Beyond Basic Training.* Council Bluffs, Iowa: T9E Publications, 1994.

Bazille, Fr., ed. *Die Kennzeichen Unserer Rassehunde.* Bielefeld, Germany: Hundesport und Jagd, n.d.

Boshell, Buris R. *Your Miniature Pinscher.* Middleburg, Virginia: Denlinger's Publishers, Ltd., 1969.

Clark, Anne Rogers and Andrew H. Brace, eds. *The International Encyclopedia of Dogs.* New York: Howell Book House, 1995.

Coile, D. Caroline, Ph.D. *Miniature Pinschers.* Hauppauge, New York: Barron's Educational Series, Inc., 1998.

Darnell, Geriane and Barbara Cecil. *Training the Competitive Small Dog.* New York: Howell Book House, 1986.

de Bylandt, Count Henry. *Dogs of All Nations.* London: Kegan Paul, Trench Trubner & Co. Ltd., 1905.

Flamholtz, Cathy J. *A Celebration of Rare Breeds.* Ft. Payne, Alabama: OTR Publications, 1986.

Leighton, Robert. *The New Book of the Dog.* London: Cassell and Co., Ltd., 1911.

Megargee, Edwin. *Dogs.* New York: Harper & Brothers, 1942.

Miller, Evelyn. *How to Raise and Train a Miniature Pinscher.* Neptune City, New Jersey: TFH Publications, Inc., 1961.

Miller, Evelyn. *Miniature Pinschers.* Neptune City, New Jersey: TFH Publications, Inc., 1990.

O'Neil, Jackie. *Guide to Owning a Miniature Pinscher.* Neptune City, New Jersey: TFH Publications, Inc., n.d.

Radel, Rose J. *The Miniature Pinscher—An Owner's Guide to a Happy, Healthy Pet.* New York: Howell Book House, 1999.

Ricketts, Viva Leone. *The Complete Miniature Pinscher.* Middleburg, Virginia: Denlinger's, 1957.

Ricketts, Viva Leone. *The Complete Miniature Pinscher,* 2nd ed. New York: Howell Book House, 1972.

Rine, Josephine. *Toy Dogs: Their History, Care and Management.* New York: Orange Judd Publishing Co., 1933.

Saunders, Blanche. *Training You to Train Your Dog.* New York: Doubleday, 1946.

Tietjen, Sari Brewster. *The New Miniature Pinscher.* New York: Howell Book House, 1988.

MONOGRAPHS

Krogh, David M. "The King of Toys Champion Book." Gresham, Oregon: Garvin Lazertype, n.d.

Krogh, David M. "Miniature Pinschers in America: A Comprehensive Record from 1958 thru 1982." Portland: Privately published, n.d.

Krogh, Sharon & David, ed. "Miniature Pinschers in America: A Comprehensive Record from 1960 thru 1969, Supplement Includes 1970." Printed by Ace Matthews Dog Shows, 1971.

Krogh, Sharon & David. "Miniature Pinschers in America: A Comprehensive Record from 1970 thru 1980." Portland: Privately published, 1980.

Miniature Pinscher Club of America:

"Everything You Ever Wanted to Know About Miniature Pinschers," n.d.

"History and Characteristics of the Miniature Pinscher," n.d.

An Illustrated Discussion of the Miniature Pinscher Standard, 1998.

"A Judges' Study Group," 1998.

Schlintz, Irene C. Khatoonian. "The Top Producers, Top Ten Group and Breed Winners: Miniature Pinschers; A Statistical and Research Presentation of Top Producers and Top Ten Groups and Breed Winners from 1965 to May 1979." Fresno, California: HIS Publications, 1979.

Zagrodnick, Barbara, ed. "Miniature Pinscher Champions and Champion Producers and Obedience Dogs and Obedience Dog Producers." Chelmsford, Massachusetts, n.d.

MAGAZINES, ARTICLES, PAMPHLETS AND BOOKLETS

AKC:

"AKC Obedience Training," pamphlet GOBED1, 1997.

"Obedience Regulations."

"Regulations for Record Keeping and Identification of Dogs," pamphlet RRRECS, 1995.

"The Right Dog for You," pamphlet GDOGO1, 1997.

"Rules Applying to Dog Shows."

"Rules Applying to Registration."

AKC Gazette: The Official Journal for the Sport of Purebred Dogs.
260 Madison Avenue
New York, NY 10016

Gaines Dog Foods, General Foods Corp.:
"The Brood Bitch and Puppies"
"First Aid for Dogs"
"Guide to Grooming"
"Welcoming Your New Puppy"

The Min Pin Monthly
Joe McGinnis, ed.
8848 Beverly Hills
Lakeland, FL 33805

Pedigree Foods. "Puppy Care Guide." Kal Kan Foods, Inc., 1998.

Pinscher Patter
Miniature Pinscher Club of America, Inc.
Jane Garvin, ed.
1922 S.W. Mawrcrest Court
Gresham, OR 97080

Purina Foods. "All About Your Puppy." Ralston Purina Co., 1991.

Top Notch Toys
Joe McGinnis, ed.
8848 Beverly Hills
Lakeland, FL 33805

Woodland PetCare Centers. "Crate Training Your Puppy," Tulsa, OK.

VIDEOTAPE

The American Kennel Club. *Miniature Pinscher.* #VVT508.
5580 Centerview Drive, Suite 200,
Raleigh, NC 27606

Index